LEADERSHIP THAT BUILDS PEOPLE

Volume II

Dr. James B. Richards

Impact International Publications
3300 N. Broad Place
Huntsville, AL 35805
(256)536-9402 • (256)536-9876
e:mail: impact4god@aol.com
website: impactministries.com

(Not affiliated with IMPACT PUBLISHERS, INC.
San Luis Obispo, California)

LEADERSHIP THAT BUILDS PEOPLE
Volume II

ISBN: 0-924748-01-7
First Printing January 1999
Printed in the United States

Published by:

Impact International Publications
3300 N. Broad Place
Huntsville, AL 35805
(256)536-9402 • (256)536-9876
e:mail: impact4god@aol.com
website: impactministries.com

Other Impact Publications:

Taking the Limits Off God
The Gospel of Peace
The Prayer Organizer
Supernatural Ministry
      Unleashing the Gifts Within You
Grace: The Power to Change
Escape from Codependent Christianity
My Church, My Family:
      How to Have a Healthy Relationship with the Church
Satan Unmasked
Foundations of Faith Workbook
Relevant Ministry Workbook
Sponsor's Workbook
Leadership that Builds People Volume I
      Developing the Heart of a Leader

Ministry Available:

Impact International School of Ministry
      Residence Program
      Correspondence
      External Degree Program
Impact Magazine (free quarterly publication)
Tape Catalog
Seminar Information
Impact of Huntsville Treatment Center

To receive any of the above, call or write today:

Impact International Publications
3300 N. Broad Place
Huntsville, AL 35805
(256)536-9402 ● (256)536-9876
e:mail: impact4god@aol.com

Impact International School of Ministry

Impact International School of Ministry is raising up leaders that are able to meet the needs of this generation. The twentieth-century church is out of touch with the real needs of society. We have become a sub-culture that speaks a language no one understands. Our methods are outdated and ineffective. We are answering the questions that no one is asking, while ignoring and minimizing the ones that are being asked.

We have become like the religious community of Jesus' day. We cling to our tradition and make the Word of God of no effect. More than once I have looked at ultra-religious people and applied this verse to them. But, the truth is, any method I cling to that is no longer effective has become my tradition.

Tradition comes from things that were good; things that worked at one time. The church is like the children of Israel who didn't want to worship in the temple because they still clung to the tabernacle. That was good, but its time had past. God's life, presence and power was no longer there. It was time to move on.

Several major sources tell us that the majority of church growth in America is actually Christians changing churches. We are not really growing. The church has become a marketing agency that competes for those who know Jesus while abandoning those who do not know Him.

Impact International School of Ministry will prepare you to reach this generation. Our commitment to the Word of God is absolute. Our commitment to methodology is as varied as the needs that exist. We are in touch with the world and we are on the cutting edge of what works.

If you are more interested in reaching the world than following the crowd, this may be the training program for you. Impact International School of Ministry has a residents program or an external program through which degrees can be earned. Call today for information:

Impact International School of Ministry
3300 N. Broad Place
Huntsville, AL 35805
(256)536-9402 ● (256)536-9876
fax: (256)536-4530
e:mail: impact4god@aol.com
website: impactministries.com

CONTENTS

Introduction

One of the most crucial events that will ever occur in an organization will be the selecting of leaders, co-workers and staff. It will be these people, more than any other factor, that will determine success or failure. These people will cause the vision to grow and expand or to die. As they represent us they will be the major factor in establishing our reputation. The world sees the leader through his/her staff. The selection or development of a leader is the most important factor in our success.

Selecting leaders is one of the seven critical factors for successful management. If effective leaders are not selected and developed, we will never move ahead to the other essential steps for success. Attempting to delegate and manage will be a nightmare if not an impossibility, with ineffective or underdeveloped leaders. Our dreams, call and future ride on the shoulders of those who surround us. Surrounded by the right people, a great leader can solve any problem, conquer any circumstance or reach any goal. Surrounded by the wrong people, it is impossible to be a great leader. Our energy and emotions will be consumed dealing with the aftermath of issues improperly handled, conflicts, insignificant decision-making and ego issues. The emotions that once propelled us toward our dream will be consumed with frustration.

No leader is stronger than those around him. The old adage, "a chain is only as strong as its weakest link," is nowhere more true than it is in a leadership team. Additionally, it is the combined strength and weakness of the team that creates the identity of an organization. Those who surround us become our five senses whereby we interpret and understand the events within our organization. To some degree, we see through their eyes and hear through their ears. Therefore, if their views are distorted, our views will be distorted. If they misunderstand, we will misunderstand. Many good decisions were made on bad information, which ultimately meant the decision was bad.

Likewise, those around us represent us. Their actions are viewed as our actions. People understand us and judge us by the actions of those who represent us. We are never independent of the image that is created by our staff. If their actions are motivated by selfish gain or egocentric needs, it will appear that those emotions are our own. Our every intention will be misrepresented through their motives.

Though staffing is very important, very few leaders are skilled at selecting and developing a staff. Too often, we are surrounded by those whose character and actions totally deny our philosophies and intentions. Those we depend on to fulfill the dream are often the very ones who make the dream an impossibility. There are critical factors essential to the success of any plan. Every situation has many different factors. However, we must learn to identify the critical factors. They are the factors crucial to success in every area of life, i.e., having a happy marriage, having a winning football team, having a great church, building a great business and having effective management.

As wise leaders we must learn the critical factors and focus our time and attention on these, leaving the rest for others. According to the 80/20 rule, 20% of our effort produces 80% of our results. This is clearly the case in dealing with critical factors. Too often we put forth valiant effort in the areas that will produce the least, all the while neglecting those things that would bring the fulfillment of our dreams. We must put our greatest effort into those factors that are critical for success.

I am very fortunate to have a wonderful marriage. When people hear me share about our marriage, they sometimes wrongly assume that Brenda and I have never had any problems. We have had some tremendous problems and have made monumental mistakes. Fortunately, however, we have not made the critical mistakes. We have discovered the critical factors for success in our relationship, and have applied them. The success of our marriage is found in commitment and effort in key areas. There are other areas not necessarily receiving the same effort. Likewise, success in business and ministry comes when we put our effort into the critical, essential areas. Success does not occur because we are proficient in every area; it is the result of being good in the critical areas.

The first critical factor of any organization is planning.[1] It is essential that we develop a realistic, workable plan. Then, we must organize to accomplish that plan. Many leaders do not have a plan and an organizational structure that is consistent. If we do not have a clear-cut plan, we will not know how to organize. The purpose of the organizational structure is to accomplish the plan. Too often, we have an idealistic, predetermined view of the "right" organizational structure. However, the right organizational structure is the one that accomplishes the plan, not the one we prefer.

Once the plan and the organizational structure have been developed, we must staff to accomplish our plan. Staffing is the process whereby we match people and specific areas of organizational goals. We must head every area of our organization with people who possess the essential skills to accomplish our plan in their area. This seems to be a consistent weakness found in most organizations. Having the right plan and the proper organizational concepts will be worthless if we do not have a staff with the appropriate skills to effectively accomplish that plan. More than once, I have faced the painful reality that I had a great plan, but did not have the right people in place to accomplish that plan. The success of every area of business and ministry is dependent upon placing the person with the appropriate skills in the appropriate area. Every time I have had an area of ministry or business that did not work, I found that I had not properly matched the leader and the task. Every time I have had an area that was functioning well, I found that successful staffing was the key.

These concepts are obvious to everyone. What is not obvious is how to select or develop these leaders. In the following pages principles are found for selecting and developing our leadership team. This book is not about methods. We select our own methods based on our leadership style and personal behavioral pattern. It is important to remember that methods are 100% variable; principles, however, are unchangeable. They transcend time, culture, leadership style and personality.[2] We can adapt our personal style to these principles and come up with a winning formula for developing an effective leadership team.

Terminology is important because of the way it influences our concepts. Therefore, I want to clarify some of the terminology I will use:

1. Staff: A staff member is anyone, paid or non-paid, who makes up your team. Among your staff will be leaders, managers and workers from every area and every level.

2. Leader: A leader is someone who heads up a particular department or task. This word is used interchangeably with the team head, head of ministry or team leader.

---

[1] Taken from a course offered through Nightingale Conant Corporation, Niles, Illinois

[2] "*Seven Habits of Highly Effective People*," Stephen R. Covey, Simon & Simon, New York

3. Team: The context will often define this word. It can sometimes refer to the entire staff or it may refer to a particular area of work or ministry. In some instances it will refer to the leadership team. Allow the context to determine the definition.

4. Leadership team: This team is comprised of a group of leaders that head up individual departments, all of whom work under the direction of a senior leader.

5. Staffing: This is the process whereby you identify, develop and hire staff members

6. Organization: When possible I use this word instead of church. These principles can be applied to any business, ministry or organization. It is important to keep that awareness. Many successful business leaders have used this information to develop a winning management team.

Too often, small churches and organizations think that the issues of staffing do not apply to them. Remember, when you place volunteers in your organization you are staffing. It is essential that you lead non-paid and paid staff by the same guidelines and principles. As you will learn, this consistency is a key to developing effective leaders. If you apply these principles, the non-paid staff of today will become your leaders of tomorrow.

1

WHERE DO YOU WANT TO GO

Successful leadership teams must have certain factors. Everyone must see the "big picture." Everyone must see the role they play in the accomplishment of the big picture. Everyone must be committed to fulfilling the common goal, along with fulfilling their personal passions.

We cannot plan, organize or staff until we know where we are going. If we want to travel the surface of the moon we will need a rocket to get there, a lunar vehicle for travel once we arrive, space suits, enough oxygen to last the entire trip, a lot of supplies and some very talented people in specific areas. If we are going across town, we simply need a Chevy with a quarter tank of gas. Until we know where we want to go, we do not know who and what it will take to get there. Planning, organization and staffing are impossible until we know where we are going.

A wonderful staff of highly trained professionals may be hired. If, however, they are not properly equipped to assist us in our specific endeavor they will not only be of no help, they will be a hindrance. A group of auto specialists can build the highest ramp in the world and the fastest car ever designed; they can be the best in their field, but if we are attempting a lunar launch, we have the wrong team. This group of highly trained professionals will cost us our life. Yes, they are good at what they do – but they are good at the wrong things.

In the beginning of any organization, it is common to find that some goals are not crystal clear. This is not altogether bad. It is common and acceptable for specific direction to develop as we proceed. However, the less clear the vision, the less probability of proper planning, organizing and staffing.[1] We only know what skills are needed to the degree that we know the destination. It is

---

[1] The "*Relevant Ministry Workbook*" explains the subtle, but essential differences between the vision, plan, organization and staffing. The vision is what we hope to accomplish in the end. The plan is what we will do to fulfil the vision. Organization is where we identify and bring together the different parts it will take to accomplish the plan. Staffing is where we place the proper person at the head of each of those organizational departments. For more details order "*The Relevant Ministry Workbook*," James B. Richards, Impact International Publications, Huntsville, Alabama

acceptable to adjust our plan as we go. However, it is not acceptable to go until we have some destination. Many times the lack of a clear-cut goal is the result of fear. The fear of failure, fear of criticism, or fear of making a mistake will only motivate us to maintain unclear goals. The person who will not commit to a specific destination is not walking in a leadership role. He is a follower. He is waiting to see where the staff is going instead of leading in a specific direction. This person cannot build a team or develop leaders. He may amass a group of people, but they will not be a team. It is not uncommon to see a church that has many sects within its congregation. Often times, each group will have opposing beliefs and a different vision. This lack of congruency becomes the cause of division and strife. It often brings about the downfall of the entire organization; the same is true in business with weak leadership.

Having a clear-cut goal may lessen the number of people who will walk with us, but it will also increase the level of commitment and team spirit. People want leadership. They want to know where the team is going. Only then can they step forward and identify how their passion can be fulfilled on our team. People without a clear-cut goal are always half-hearted and reluctant. They lack passion, drive and purpose.

The paradox of staffing is found in this reality: every person must fulfill their individual passion, and every person must be fully committed to the goals of the team. This produces a synergy that exceeds anything we could accomplish alone. In a synergistic environment, two or more factors come together, maintain their individual function and identity, all the while becoming something they could never be alone. It is the absence of synergy that creates a centrifugal energy that scatters instead of gathers. It pulls any organization in opposing directions giving rise to weakness, division and destruction.

When we bring staff into a leadership position, it is essential that their passion and goals be consistent with ours. They must be able to fulfill their passion while fulfilling ours. They are, after all, becoming a part of a team. A group of men wearing the same uniform do not make a football team. They must all run toward the same goal. They have to be good at playing a specific position. They have to know the plays. Working together they create synergy. They each play a different position that they love, but everyone has the same purpose.

As a leader, there is a fine line between control and leading. We never want to dominate. We never want to misuse people. Yet, we must fulfill our passion. How we build our team will force us to be a controller or a leader. Knowing where we are going and selecting people who have a passion for the area in which they are needed is the key to never becoming a controller.

There will always be people who want to be a part of our team. We must be wise enough to make good personnel decisions. We must have a process whereby we identify and prove a person's skill, passion and character. This is for our good as well as theirs. Everyone does not need to be on our team. Regardless of how talented and skilled, they may be the wrong person for the job. It is better to have a less talented, passionate person in the right spot than to have a very talented, passionless person in the wrong spot. An unfulfilled person always becomes trouble. It has been said, "One person with a passion is greater than ninety-nine with only interest."[1]

Too often people are brought into a position because of their personal loyalty to the leader. This is an environment that breeds codependency and deceit. A wise leader wants people who have a high commitment to their own passion. I do not want a leader on my team who would abandon his/her passion to be on my staff. Likewise, the leader who has foresight wants each team member to be more committed to the goal than to the leader. A person who is committed to the cause will be faithful whether I am present or absent. The secure leader realizes the importance of personal commitment, but recognizes where such commitment ranks on the priority scale. Personal commitment is certainly not at the top of the list for a leader who is committed to the plan.

We often allow our fears, insecurities and ambitions to control us. Out of greed, we want everyone on our team. We do not want to let the good ones go, so we "trouble our own house." We undermine our own dream. We put good people in the wrong slots. We think we can change them. We attempt to manipulate their passions. We think we can make them faithful to our dreams. Time always reveals - a person who is willing to be untrue to his own dreams can never be trusted with our dreams. Regard-

---

[1] Source Unknown.

less of the skill and talent, a person's passion must be consistent with ours. They must want the same end result that we want. They are not wrong if they do not want to fulfill our passion. They are just not right for us. Not every person is going to be the quarterback. Not every person is going to carry the ball, but everyone on the team has to love football and want to win. It is absolutely essential that they see how they could fulfill their passions by becoming a part of our team. We should not coerce a fast basketball player into carrying the ball for us. Every time we think he is about to score, he will try dribbling the ball. They need to play the game and position they desire, not the one we desire for them. Too many times, talented people have been asked to give up their dream for ours. That is completely wrong. We should never ask a person to give up their dream. Our dream will not motivate them. Its accomplishment will not fulfill them. They will become the one who requires constant encouragement and motivation. They will be the one who wants to quit every time it gets hard. They are the ones who are never really with us.

The common complaint I hear from leaders and managers around the world is, "I cannot get the people to be diligent and committed. I cannot find people who have a passion for anything." Too often, inquiry reveals that the person is being motivated to do something he really does not want to do. The leader wanted him to do it! Herein we find the difference between a manipulator and a motivator. A manipulator encourages others to do what he desires. A motivator encourages others to do what they desire.

Too often, a leader makes everyone feel that they must share his/her specific passion. We insist that they must love what we love. That environment produces guilt, condemnation and frustration. "If I do not want what the leader wants, there must be something wrong with me." They not only fail to have a passion for our dreams, they lose passion for their own dreams. We become the "dream stealer" by exalting our dreams above the dreams of others. Once we have stolen their dream they will become frustrated, passionless people doomed for failure. Their failure will contribute to our failure. In the end our selfish ambitions prevent us all from living our dreams.

As a leader with integrity, we must first know where we are going. We must have a plan to get there. We must organize around that plan. And we must staff to meet those organizational needs. Those staff members, whether volunteer or paid staff, must have a vision that will compliment ours. Likewise, our vision must facilitate the fulfillment of theirs.

Proverbs 22:6 says, *"Train up a child in the way he should go: and when he is old, he will not depart from it."* The way he should go is according to his particular bent or desire. Too many parents manipulate their children into fulfilling the parents' desire. Thus, we have unmotivated children in school. College becomes a playground and drugs provide the fulfillment that is not being found in life. The majority of adults in America are not satisfied with their current occupation. They would do something else if they had the opportunity to do it over. There is no wonder there is such apathy in the work place.

Just as a parent should encourage a child to fulfill his own passions, a benevolent leader will seek to know and understand the passions of those he leads. He will seek to place those people in an area where their personal passion is fulfilled. It becomes a win-win situation. The staff member wins because he gets to fulfill his dream. The leader and the organization win because their goal is fulfilled. All of this is the product of knowing where we are going and finding those who can walk with us while fulfilling their dream.

Questions for the heart:

1. Do I really know what my vision is?

2. Do I have a plan to get there? If so, write out the plan.

3. Have I allowed other successful people to critique my plan?

4. Have I identified the various organizational factors I need?

5. Have I added staff to meet my organizational goals, or have I built my organization around available talent?

6. Do I know the vision of each of my leaders and team members? If not, talk with them and write it down.

7. Will each of my leaders/team members be able to fulfill their vision and stay true to my vision?

8. Who should not be a part of this team?

9. Which leaders require constant motivation? From what I now know, is it a character issue or a staffing issue?

10. Am I committed to the success of each member of my team?

2

LIFE PHILOSOPHY

The way we manage our organization is ultimately an extension of our personal life philosophies. It is essential that there be congruence in our life philosophies, business philosophies and the leadership philosophies of our team. This lack of congruence[1] sends a mixed message to those whom we desire to serve, whether the customer or the congregation.

It is essential that the leadership team embrace the same philosophies as the leader. Otherwise, there will be inconsistency in the way people are treated. This inconsistency is sometimes more destructive than a consistently negative philosophy. People want to know what to expect. They do not want to think very much. They want things to be predictable. Inconsistency among the leadership will result in an inconsistent message and method of human relations.

In *"Leadership That Builds People, Volume I,"* we discussed the primary question a leader must ask him/herself. *Will I use the people to build my ministry, or will I use the ministry to build people?*[2] Those who find the secret to serving the needs of humanity are the ones who find true success. They are the ones who contribute to the quality of life of others. In church, business and life, we are either a giver or a taker. It is in this very issue that our personal philosophies are revealed.

We ignorantly embrace a dichotomy about life issues. We think that in every relationship there will always be one who wins and one who loses. It seems impossible that both can win. One of us must lose. It is this incorrect rationale that justifies our mistreatment of others. It is this concept that justifies the company's abuse of employees. It is this error that allows the salesman to exaggerate to the harm of the customer. It is this paradigm

---

[1] In this context congruency speaks of consistency of purpose, action and intention wherein all parts work together for the same goals.

[2] *"Leadership That Builds People, Volume I"* is an essential prerequisite for utilizing the information in this book. It provides the basis from which all healthy leadership can emerge. This book is written from the position that the leadership principles in Volume I are accepted.

that justifies the church using people for its own purpose. A good deal is only good when everyone wins. When two people want the same thing, both may not get everything they want, but no one has to lose. Every principle and procedure that Jesus established screamed this reality. Yet, it has fallen on the deaf ear of a politically motivated, egocentric church that believes the end justifies the means. We have abandoned the principle of selflessness and embraced self-centeredness. After we win, we still lack peace, joy and personal fulfillment. This emptiness drives us to the further exploitation of our fellow man.

For years in business and in ministry, I have found myself surrounded by those who gave lip service to my convictions. As long as we were making money in business or growing in ministry, everyone wanted to walk in love and kindness. When the chips were down, however, they reverted back to the self-centered leadership style that denied everything I believed. The self-centered leader will put forth all of the actions of love, as long as it gets the desired response. It is not the action that determines if something is love, it is the action and the intent. Love acts in a certain manner even when there is no personal gain. Too many times the actions of these people resulted in an inconsistent message being sent to the congregation or customer, which reflected negatively on my character.

It has been said that when verbal and non-verbal communications contradict, people always believe the non-verbal. It is "how we say it" that effects people more than what we say. Likewise, when our staff represents us in a manner inconsistent with our positions, the majority of the people will not believe the validity of our words. The inconsistency between our actions and those of our staff will lead them to assume we are deceivers.

To determine congruence, we can start by writing our vision statement. Our vision statement should describe the thing we hope to accomplish in our business or ministry. Then, we should write out our mission statement. This statement tells how we will accomplish the vision. For example, "We believe we will build a church of _____ that will effect the way the world sees God." That is our vision. Our mission statement says, "We intend to reach the lost, the backslidden, the unchurched and the unproductive, and make them whole through the love of God, and launch them into productive, personal service." This tells how we will fulfill the vision. Then we must identify our philosophy of human relations. "We will never use control or manipulation. In all that we do we will seek to build a Biblically-based sense of self-worth. We will never intentionally hurt a person's self-worth. We will endeavor to bring every person into a responsible, personal relationship with God and others." This human relations statement becomes the boundaries within which we must accomplish the vision and live the mission.

For true congruence we must now identify our life philosophies. What do we value in life? What is important to us? As several have asked, "If today were my funeral and people were walking by my casket, what would I want my family and friends to say?" I have personally redefined this several times over the years. At this point, I would want my family and friends to say, "Jim always made me feel loved, and he always made me believe that God loved me." That is my life vision.

Once we have identified our life vision we must *consider our ways*! We must ask ourselves, "Am I managing my life and relationships in a way that will accomplish this life vision?" So we must identify our own personal mission statement and our philosophy of human relations.[3] Now comes the challenging question. Is all of this congruent? Again, we must ask ourselves, "Will the way I manage my personal life make people feel loved?" The quantum leap comes, however, when we have determined whether our philosophy statements for business and ministry are consistent with our life philosophies. Too many Christians are sheep at church and wolves at work. Everything we believe must permeate every area of our life or it causes deep, internal stress and conflict.

Until we have resolved these issues, we have no hope of building a leadership team that has congruence. We cannot lead others until we know where we are going in personal life and in ministry or business. When we have defined and committed ourselves to our life's philosophies, we open our heart to God in a way that allows Him to lead us along a path that is devoid of conflict and turmoil. When our business or ministry objectives conflict with our personal objectives, our heart hardens and our life philosophies are lost. We should want our life, ministry and business to be surrounded by people whose goals and

---

[3] *"Relevant Ministry Workbook,"* James B. Richards, Impact International Publications, Huntsville, Alabama

philosophies are consistent with ours. These people will have different strengths and weaknesses - they will do things differently. They will see things from a different perspective, but these people will be internally guided by the same principles that guide our lives.

Too many times we staff our leadership team with those who give lip service to our business or ministry philosophies, yet their lifestyle is in total contradiction. A person will always revert back to true lifestyle beliefs, especially under pressure. Therefore, we know that a man will treat the customer or congregation the same way he treats his wife and children. We do not know who they will be on our team until we know who they are at home.[4] The number one trust factor we must resolve for them to be on our leadership team is this: "Can I trust you with the people?" The answer to that question determines if they are right for our leadership team. Only then can we consider if they have the personal skills to lead a particular area of the organization.

I do not want a leader who uses negative motivation with his family. That philosophy will seep into the ministry. A man who justifies controlling his wife will justify controlling God's people.

The life philosophy will always rule over the business/ministry philosophies. Regardless of our verbal commitment and lofty ideas, apart from a healthy life philosophy there will not be healthy ministry.

---

[4] We will address this in more detail in the section dealing with qualifications.

Questions for the heart:

1. Write your vision statement. What do you want to accomplish?

2. Write your mission statement. How do you want to accomplish this?

3. Write your philosophy of human relations.

4. Write your life's philosophy.

   A. What do I value in life?
   B. What is important to me?
   C. If today were my funeral, what would I want my friends and/or family to say?
   D. Am I managing my life in a manner that accomplishes this?

5. Is all of the above congruent with my present lifestyle?

6. Does the way I currently manage my life make others feel loved?

7. Meet and discuss your philosophies with all of your staff. Allow them to express their views on each of these points.

3

LIKE-MINDED LEADERS

Having leaders who are of one mind and purpose is absolutely essential. Being like-minded does not mean that we agree on everything. It does not mean that we have the same behavior patterns. It means that we are in agreement in the essential areas. I highly value the diversity of my staff. I want to be surrounded by people who think differently than I. If we all see everything the same, we have too many weaknesses and blind spots. Our diversity of perception and opinion is a great strength. A strong leader is never threatened by differences of opinion.

A leadership team does not function like a denomination or political party. We do not exist to maintain or reinforce our opinions. It is not about providing strength for weak leaders who need the false security of agreement. Mature leaders will surround themselves with those who know how to challenge and disagree in a mature way. "Yes men" are the destruction of too many organizations. A healthy leadership team will nurture and challenge one another. Their commitment to the cause prevents them from being "yes men."

I remember being called upon for consultation work with a particular ministry leader. He had a key spot in his ministry that he could not keep filled. Every time he found a person who seemed to be right for the job, he would soon discover that their weaknesses made them unacceptable for the position. He was a typical insecure leader who did not like to be challenged. He was accustomed to surrounding himself with those who would always agree with him. My advice to him was simple, "When you find someone who has the basic skills, he will probably be someone you will not like on a personal level. The skills needed to fill this slot will not be found in a typical 'yes man.' You are making the decisions for this person. Therefore, he is not able to do his job. The reason he agrees with all of your decisions is because he is just like you. You both see everything the same. That means you both have the same weaknesses. You both have the same blind spots. You both forget the same things. You both make the same mistakes. Stop hiring people to be your buddy. Hire someone who has the skill to do the job -

a job you or someone like you does not have the skill to do."

Once we get passed the fact that we want diversity and we know that the person has the qualifications, we must be sure that we are like-minded in the crucial areas. More than anything else, we want to know that the person will be a servant to the people. We want to know that they will always seek what is best for the people. Paul had this same concern when he wrote to the Philippian church. "*But I trust in the Lord Jesus to send Timotheus shortly unto you, that I also may be of good comfort, when I know your state. For I have no man likeminded, who will naturally care for your state. For all seek their own, not the things which are Jesus Christ's.*" Philippians 2:19-21.

In every area of life, ministry, and business leaders must be willing to seek the care of those they serve. Otherwise, we are not leaders at all; we are simply self-centered controllers. Remember, I am not saying that we should lose and they should win. I am saying we should all win. In every situation every person should walk away having benefited themselves and others. We must have leaders whom we know will serve the people. This is an area where I have experienced my greatest tragedy and disappointment. This is where I have learned the hardest leadership lessons. We all agree, in theory, that we want our staff to be like-minded. I have always known what I wanted in my leaders. I just did not know how to identify those traits. Experience has proven that I can rarely bring in a person from the outside who has my same value for people. As I stated earlier, I often find those who eagerly agree with my teaching about serving and leading. I find those who say the same things I say, but in practice, they tend to revert to control and manipulation.

One of the great weaknesses of most organizations is in development and promotion of leaders. We must have a system of developing leaders that is balanced with didactic[1] training, modeling, supervised application and on-going development. We must have a staff that is highly qualified in their particular skills, yet fully committed to serving.

Everyone looks good on paper. Too many times

---

[1] Didactic training is primarily instructional. While it is essential, it has as its goal the transferring of information. The church has limited most of its training to verbal instruction, which is easily misunderstood and has no character development at all.

the application and the references are a far cry from reality. We must accept the undeniable reality: If we desire a leadership team that is committed to serving God and His people we must develop them. Few schools, colleges, seminaries or churches actually train anyone to serve.

Like-minded leaders are developed through a consistent, systematic, developmental program. Even those who come with all of the proper credentials and saying all the right things usually require development. By patiently applying these principles we will find ourselves surrounded by a diverse group of people who are committed to the same cause and are governed by the same values; yet, they maintain their individual identity and passion.

NOTES

Questions for the heart:

1. Do you currently have a diversified group of staff/leaders?

2. Did you select your current leaders more for social rapport or because their skills match the organizational needs?

3. Do the people around me seem to be one behavior type?

4. Do we tend to see things differently or the same?

5. Do those differences produce strife or growth?

6. In which areas does your ministry/organization lack? This is sometimes best identified by the criticism of your organization.

7. Do we have the diversity to fill the areas we lack? Or, do the team members always justify your current positions?

8. Do you have a system of developing leaders/staff to insure that you are all like-minded?

9. Is it clear to all of your staff that your organization exists to serve and develop God's people?
   A. In your next staff meeting have each person with no prompting to write what they think are the top five priorities for your organization.
   B. See how congruent these are with your priorities.

NOTES

SECTION 2

<u>DEVELOPING LEADERS</u>

The process whereby we develop leaders is a reflection of our understanding of the needs and objectives of our organization and our team members. As a senior leader I must adopt a leadership philosophy that says, "All problems are leadership problems." If the buck really stops here, then I must accept that I am the only one who has the responsibility, the opportunity and the means to bring about any needed change. If I am surrounded by weak leaders, it is either a product of my selection process or development process. In either case, I am the one who can do something about it.

Responsibility is not about blame. Blame looks to the problem. Responsibility looks to the solution. Blame focuses on the past, responsibility focuses on the future. Blame is reactive; responsibility is proactive. The one who is responsible is the one who can do something about the problem.[1] One of the true marks of a leader is found in his ability and willingness to accept responsibility and become proactive.

To have the "dream team" we must become proactive. We must accept the responsibility for the choices we have made. We must quit finding excuses and find solutions. We must create a process whereby we develop responsible, caring leaders. If our present leadership team is not effective we must develop a plan that gives the opportunity to become more effective. If they cannot be developed we should replace them. A true leader accepts the challenge of dismissing a person in a way that maintains integrity.

In this section we will explore the process of developing effective leaders.

---

[1] "*Escape from Codependent Christianity*," James B. Richards, Impact International Publications, Huntsville, Alabama

4

NOT ANOTHER PROGRAM

If, in our home, we have a leaking roof, it is no real problem to put on a new one. If our walls have holes, they are easily repaired. If, however, the foundation is bad, we have a serious problem. Usually, the entire structure must be torn down and rebuilt. God's commission to Jeremiah the prophet was to tear down and put up, so He could plant. *"See, I have this day set thee over the nations and over the kingdoms, to root out, and to pull down, and to destroy, and to throw down, to build, and to plant."* Jeremiah 1:10.

A ministry organization that does not have developing people as its primary goal is built on a faulty foundation.[1] When we serve people with God's Word and love, we are serving God. This is not a wall or roof being replaced. This is the foundation. This is the determining factor of our existence. Unfortunately, most ministries have built upon a purpose that is not compatible with the Biblical concept of servant-leadership and personal development. Those ministries have been staffed with people who are not motivated by the desire to serve and develop others. Too often, the entire agenda for the average American ministry is to succeed, not to be effective.[2] In this environment, the organization is simply a machine that exists to keep itself alive. It is like a shark that must keep moving to live, so they have to eat to keep moving. It is a never-ending cycle of self-perpetuation. Before too long, the original goals and concepts are lost in the need to survive at the current level of perceived success.

Our faulty paradigm of success locks us into a "stuck state." In his description of the "stuck state," Paul Scheele describes it as that state where one oscillates between what he wants and what he fears.[3] The Bible calls this wavering or double-minded. As one prophet said,

---

[1] The same is true for a business that does not see the need to serve the customer.

[2] In "*Leadership That Builds People Volume I, Devleoping the Heart of a Leader,*" we discuss the three different kinds of churches: growing churches, stuck churches and effective churches. It may be good to review at this time.

[3] "*Natural Brilliance,*" Paul R. Scheele, M.A., Learning Strategies Corporation, Wayzata, Minnesota

"How long halt ye between two opinions?"   We will only break free from the stuck state when we have the assurance that we will not lose the present positive benefits. Too often, our concepts of success and serving presents a dichotomy that paralyzes us. We fear that serving will rob us of our feelings of success.

The internal destruction that leads to the corruption of many organizations and individuals is born from this faulty belief system. Our organizations only have the right to exist for the purpose of ministering to people. We only deserve to grow to the degree that we contribute to the quality of people's lives. When we no longer exist for these purposes, we become users and destroyers. Developing workers and leaders who exist to serve God's people rather than control God's people requires a major rethinking of structure, philosophy and leadership style.   An attempt to build this onto an existing foundation will probably bring about the collapse of the entire structure.

I see the church as a living organism that fulfills the great commission to the world and the great commission of the five-fold ministry. We must reach the world with the message of God's love, salvation, righteousness and peace. The world must know what Jesus has done. This is our commission to the world. *"And Jesus came and spake unto them, saying, All power is given unto me in heaven and in earth. Go ye therefore..."* This does not, however, represent the entirety of the commission given to the church.   This only represents the initial phase of our commission. We are then told to teach, i.e, make disciples of those who receive our Word. *"Go ye therefore, and teach all nations, baptizing them in the name of the Father, and of the Son, and of the Holy Ghost: Teaching them to observe all things whatsoever I have commanded you: and, lo, I am with you alway, even unto the end of the world. Amen."* Matthew 28:19-20.

The process of making disciples far exceeds outward legalistic compliance to a set of rules. This discipling process is to be modeled more than it is to be told. We are to "disciple them to observe all that Jesus taught." This is not about the mere regurgitation of information for which the twentieth-century church has become so famous. This is not about bringing people under our control. This is about relating to people and laying down our life for them just as Jesus did for His disciples. The Bible provides the boundaries within which we must disciple those we reach.

NOTES

The commission to the overseers is to equip, mend and make whole the saints, so they can do the work of the ministry and build up the body. The concept of serving was established by God Himself and demonstrated through the ministry of Jesus. It was given as a commission to the leaders. It is to be the lifestyle of the people. Every office in the church is a position from which we serve in a manner that will fulfill Jesus' commission to the leaders of the church.

As we learn the teachings of the Lord Jesus and come into a meaningful relationship with God, through Him, we are made whole. We are mended from the hurts and pains that have been inflicted upon us. We are set free from the bondage of fear by the love of God. When serving is our goal, we are free from the temptation to control. These two antithetical motivations can never inter-mingle. You cannot control and serve.

Our paradigm of ministry must be clearly defined and developed in our leadership team. Failure to teach, model and develop Biblical leadership concepts will result in chaos and downfall. Jesus left us with a leadership commission. There is no other commission for healthy leadership. *"And he gave some, apostles; and some, prophets; and some, evangelists; and some, pastors and teachers; For the perfecting of the saints, for the work of the ministry, for the edifying of the body of Christ."* Ephesians 4:11-12. This is the agenda we must breed into each potential leader. Every leader must be thoroughly prepared to serve God's people, help them become whole and help them find their place of service.

The phrase, "perfecting the saints," literally means to mend and equip. It is the same Greek word used when speaking of "mending tattered and torn fishing nets."[4] Our job is not to control or to make right. Our God-given commission is to mend and make whole to the extent that every believer becomes equipped to do the work of the ministry and edify the body of Christ. There should be a never-ending cycle of evangelizing, emotional and physi-cal healing, discipling, equipping and developing new leaders. Therefore, our organization should be set up to accomplish this goal. Regardless of the particular empha-sis of our ministry, these elements must be present for us to

---

[4] *"Supernatural Ministry: Unleashing the Gifts Within You,"* James B. Richards, Impact International Publications, Huntsville, Alabama

accomplish the call of God.

The style of government we choose is non-essential. It is the motive and the purpose of our governmental style that is essential. For too long we have majored on non-essential issues to the neglect of the call of God upon the church and its leaders. We must accept and model the same purposes that Jesus modeled. We must work the same plan. The Holy Spirit is not here to work our plan and glorify us in the earth. He is here to glorify God through the plan that Jesus gave.

This process of evangelizing, healing, discipling and equipping can only continue to happen if we have a system that develops leaders in the process. Developing leaders should not be some separate, isolated process. It should be a part of the continuum of developing people. Too often we have programs that are not congruent in nature. They create too many loose ends. They do not all point toward and accomplish the same goal or destination. Every program should move people progressively along the lines of personal and/or spiritual development and the development of a servant's mentality. The same program that gets them saved should hold the seeds of leadership development.

A servant's mentality is not one of low self-worth. It is one of honor, dignity and worth. Those who serve from low self-worth are not servants. They are slaves! Only when we serve from a sense of sonship and ownership will there be healthy personal development.[5] We must also realize that a servant's mentality is not about serving the organization; it is about serving people through the organization. We must develop a paradigm that honors the servant not the ruler. Jesus said, "*The disciple is not above his master, nor the servant above his lord. It is enough for the disciple that he be as his master, and the servant as his lord. Matthew 10:24-25a. For even the Son of man came not to be ministered unto, but to minister, and to give his life a ransom for many.*" Mark 10:45.

---

[5] Galatians 4:4-7, "*But when the time had fully come, God sent his Son, born of a woman, born under law, to redeem those under law, that we might receive the full rights of sons. Because you are sons, God sent the Spirit of his Son into our hearts, the Spirit who calls out, 'Abba, Father.' So you are no longer a slave, but a son; and since you are a son, God has made you also an heir.*" See "*Dignity and Worth*," James B. Richards, Impact International Publications, Huntsville, Alabama

Everything we teach and model should make people whole. It should move them toward a life that revolves around the same purposes of Jesus. It should be enough, to be like our Lord and Master! This should be at the core of motivation for every activity. This motive should be the seed that conceives and guides every program.

Developing effective leaders cannot simply be one of many programs. It cannot be an afterthought. Our churches should have one program that progressively developes people's character. Where they stop in that process should be their choice. It should not be the result of reaching the limitations of our program. Actually, the character traits of leaders are the same as those that should be sought by all believers. There should not be one standard for leaders and another for "regular believers." A program that develops people will succeed at whatever level the person allows themselves to be developed.

Questions for the heart:

Answer the following questions to determine if you must establish a new foundation for your organization:

1. Do your leaders serve the organization or the people?

2. Do your leaders ever feel that control is acceptable, especially when a person seems incapable of making right choices?

3. Is your leadership training program focused on the organization or the people?

4. Do the people in your church tend to serve others freely, or do they seek to be served?

5. Do you feel that serving the people would make them too self-centered?

6. Would your leadership team have the freedom to question you if they perceived selfish motives in your actions?

7. Is serving and developing people the core motivation for all that your ministry does?

8. Are your various programs a continuum or do they tend to have different, unrelated objectives?

9. Are those who rule bestowed more honor than those who serve?

5

ESTABLISHING A SYSTEM

Once it is determined exactly who we are serving, the organization or the people, we know how to establish a system that will develop leaders who are truly servants. Keep in mind, the organization does not lose because we serve the people. If, in fact, it is our desire to build a church modeled after the Biblical pattern, the organization and the people will greatly benefit from this process.

For a number of years I had difficulty raising up "second generation" leaders. I could successfully develop first generation leaders, but they were not successfully developing leaders. At first I blamed the leaders. In time I had to accept the obvious. There was something in my plan that was not congruent with the objectives. In time, I identified my two main weaknesses.

My first weakness lay in the fact that I had no absolute way of identifying and separating those who "walk the walk" from those who "talk the talk." Developing leaders is much like dating. When a guy wants a girl he can fake it for a long time. So it is with those who desire to be leaders. There must be a way of proving those who express a desire to serve on my team without violating principles of integrity and without pushing people into a performance mentality.

The second weakness of my system was that it did not provide a natural progression of development that started the day people walked through my doors, all the way through to them finding a place to serve. There was a lack of congruence in my programs. My system was not a continuum. It was various assorted programs that all had the same goal, but did not flow from one stage to the other in a natural progression.

Adopting a Biblical model of leadership development easily solved both problems. Jesus gave us a pattern of developing leaders. It included didactic training, modeling, supervision, teamwork, reporting, rewards and ongoing leadership development. All of these facets were a part of a single system wherein each of these elements formed a part of the continuum from belief to leadership.[1]

---

[1] "*Relevant Ministry Workbook,*" James B. Richards, Impact International Publications, Huntsville, Alabama

Too often we develop leaders in a vacuum, i.e., the classroom.[2] Anything can seem normal in isolation. We evaluate their knowledge to perform a task, but we do not have a system that provides us with the opportunity to evaluate and develop their people skills in action. We do not really know their commitment to our values. We have not seen how they resolve conflict. We do not know if they really care about the people. Anyone can put the right answers on a test, but the real question is this, "Have they turned those answers into beliefs, attitudes and skills that work in a real life setting?"

Jesus had the perfect system for developing leaders. He taught the Word of God. He gave them the information they needed. The second step is key, He then modeled what He taught. This, in my estimation, is the number one breakdown of leadership in our society. We tell people what we want them to do, but they never see us do it. This is a main cause for so much fear. People fear the unknown. It is still unknown until it has been seen.

In our School of Ministry[3] we have had the opportunity to observe and evaluate the difference between our correspondence students and our resident students. We have found that both groups can follow the same course of study and embrace the same theological positions. Yet, the correspondence students seldom really grasp the spirit of our program. The correspondence students do not have the opportunity to sit in our church, observe our leaders and see how we apply the realities of servant leadership. They pass the tests, believe the same doctrines, but apply different life principles.

For nearly fifteen years we have seen that the major change happens during a student's second year. The second year curriculum is more participation than information. It is not learning new information that brings the transformation. It is the implementation! Jesus did not just say, *"The truth will set you free."* He said, *"If ye continue in my word, then are ye my disciples indeed; And ye shall know the truth, and the truth shall make you free."*

---

[2] The classroom is the cornerstone of twentieth-century teaching. Yet, the classroom only provides didactic teaching, which is the least effective form of personal development. Personal growth starts with hearing, progresses to believing and is proven in the doing.

[3] Impact International School of Ministry, Huntsville, Alabama

John 8:31-32. It is becoming a disciple; believing and walking in (continuing/applying) truth that sets one free. The Jews argued that they were free just because they were children of Abraham. That is much like the Christian who lives in bondage, has been given freedom, but in practice is still bound. All the while insisting that because he is saved, he has complete freedom. From God's perspective, freedom is his. It was provided at the cross. That is of little value, however, until it is realized and experienced in real life. In this case it is the one with a call on his/her life that says I am a minister, but in practice they do not know how to make that functional. The call does not equate the "know how."

Jesus modeled the principles of life, as well as the principles of ministry. He modeled the reality that everyone was important to Him. After the disciples heard the teaching about the Kingdom of God, they still would have turned the children away. They saw Him take the time to minister to the children. After they heard Him proclaim healing for all, they tried to silence the blind man who cried out for healing. They heard the message, but had not developed the heart of a servant. Jesus continually modeled what He taught.

It is in the modeling that we see the realities. I remember being in a service where a man stood up and brought a completely irrational prophecy. The man had an emotional disorder. I will never forget the gentleness and wisdom the pastor used to deal with that situation. I saw how to meld together the realities of authority and mercy. I saw what could have been a devastating situation for the person and the church turned into an opportunity for ministry. To this day the way that situation was handled has effected the way I have publicly handled difficult public situations. I could not have gotten that from a textbook.

After Jesus allowed them to see Him implement the Word, He gave them opportunity to minister. Too many times they failed, as in the case of the demoniac. He then gave instructions and modeled the solution. People need to be observed and have immediate, loving but relevant, feedback about their performance. While it is fresh on their mind, they need to ask the questions that are stirred by the situation.

Next, He sent them out in teams to minister together. They now had the opportunity to go out on their own and put it all into practice. In this setting they would correct their own mistakes. They would learn to listen to God for themselves. But, they were not alone. They had someone with them. I assume that one may have always been more experienced than the other. People are stronger and more confident when ministering with another.[4] They are much more apt to follow the plan when there is emotional support and accountability.

Then the disciples came back and reported all that had transpired. It was a time of reward, and acknowledgement. Sharing experiences and testimonies is a healthy part of development. It is also a great opportunity for further development. Not only is their instruction from the teacher, but their is instruction from the peers.

The disciples then continued with Jesus. As they observed Him they fine-tuned their methods. One only knows which questions to ask and what to look for when they have had personal experience. Many of our School of Ministry students have years of ministry experience, some are fresh out of high school. There is a great gap between the types of questions asked by the two groups. Those who have had experience ask relevant questions. Their experience guides their learning process. Those with no experience do not yet know what they should ask. Training after experience is where the true skills are developed. At this point one knows what to look for; what questions to ask.

When people walk through our doors, they have entered a true realm of equal opportunity. Anyone who wants to follow the leader can. Like Jesus, and the twelve disciples, we occasionally choose some. For the most part, however, "whosoever will" can follow.

Their desire to follow the leader of their choice and how far they desire to follow them will determine how far they go. Every leader is capable of taking a new believer through this process of instruction, modeling, supervision, teamwork, reporting, rewards and ongoing supervision. It is one congruent continuum.

Developing a system that incorporates the Biblical model of leadership development will produce the desired results. It will develop mature, experienced, responsible leaders. At this point it would be advisable to establish the trail of congruency within your program. Following are some suggestions that will help.

---

[4] *"Supernatural Ministry: Unleashing the Gifts Within You,"* James B. Richards, Impact International Publications, Huntsville, Alabama

Questions for the heart:

1. Take the mission statement from every department in your organization and place in the sequence that a person will be exposed to them. Then read those statements. Do they all cause a person to reach the same destination with a servant's attitude?

2. Do I have a training program?

3. Does my program provide congruency and consistency?

4. Evaluate your training process and identify the following:

    A. Do you have a place where potential leaders receive meaningful didactic training? If so, evaluate all of that material and determine if it promotes a servant's attitude.

    B. Is too much of our program based on the mere exchange of information?

    C. Do you have a regular system of modeling the things you teach?

    D. If so:
        i. Where and how does this happen?
        ii. Is it meaningful?
        iii. Is there a deliberate plan to model what we teach?

    E. Do potential leaders have opportunity to implement what they are learning under supervision? Does that supervision provide prompt, positive evaluation and correction?

    F. Do we put them in teams and give them freedom to minister?

    G. Do they report back to share their experiences?

    H. Do we provide ongoing training and leadership?

    I. Do we provide rewards in the form of acknowledgement and appreciation?

6

DEVELOPING RELEVANT LEADERS

Servants and leaders are developed more than they are discovered. Because of the codependent nature of our society, responsible people are scarce. Effective leaders are even harder to find. This plague is not unique to the church, but is also a continual affliction to the business world. It is harder than ever to find well-developed, responsible people; therefore, we must develop them. If we are to minister to the relevant needs of our society, we must develop leaders who have our commitment to God, love people and are in touch with the current needs of those they seek to serve. We must develop them morally, emotionally and spiritually as well as cultivate their leadership skills.

Many Seminaries and Bible Colleges are out of touch with the current needs of society. Their teachers are theoretical theologians who seldom prove their theories in real life. Many who were once very effective are so out of touch with the mainstream of society that they do not have a clue what it will take to be effective in ministry today. When those graduates step into our program, they are placed in the same program as a new convert to develop their leadership skills. They may progress at a faster pace, but they are all in the same system. Very often, the new convert will be more effective than the trained minister because he understands the current trends of society.

I recently took several people from our church to an excellent leadership conference. The speaker was tremendous. I will take other church members to similar conferences. During the break I met with my people to talk about what we had heard thus far. I quickly realized that I must help them understand the perspective that was being taught. If the average person we win to the Lord is a "1" and becoming an effective leader is a "10," we must realize that what he is explaining assumes that the people who come into our church are already "4's" or "5's."

Society has changed. Our judicial system no longer holds people responsible for their actions. Students graduate from high school who cannot read because they are never held responsible. Unions and government regulations often make it impossible to enforce high work standards. The quality of the American work force has been in continual declined for years. Government leaders attempt to buy votes by offering life with no responsibilities. Our country thrives on codependency. The entire world's system is one that nurtures codependency and irresponsibility.[1] It is for this very reason that the Bible teaches us to free ourselves from the conforming power of the world's system.[2]

For this reason every segment of society is suffering. Good employees are harder to find. The stable segment of society is shrinking year by year. Therefore, the church that will endure must be committed to reaching and developing people as never before. This is a timely process that the modern church is not equipped or willing to face. Like the early Sunday Schools that taught people to read, the church can meet this need in society that is overlooked by the world's system of education.

Twenty years ago you could win someone to Jesus and if they were serious about God, you had someone who would serve and grow into a leadership position fairly quickly. Any new convert was a person who usually had some work skills. They understood responsibility. They were usually an asset to the church from the first day. Today when you reach a new convert, it is rare that person will have many social or work skills. If they do possess meaningful skills, they are so steeped in self-centeredness that it takes time to develop a sense of responsibility toward the local church.

American culture has become the accepted norm. Our theologians attempt to confirm and prove our selfish value system through the Word of God. Our culture is one that glorifies the individual. There is no realization of synergy. Healthy nationalism is a foreign concept. It matters not how the group suffers if the individual is gratified. This is the age of self. Thus, there is little loyalty, commitment or integrity.

The church is now put into a place where we must not only teach spiritual values, we must cultivate a work ethic, the value of commitment and other areas of personal responsibility. All of this must happen before the new convert ever gets to the place where we can depend on them for much of anything. Most of our converts are going

---

[1] *"Escape from Codependent Christianity,"* James B. Richards, Impact International Publications, Huntsville, Alabama

[2] Romans 12:2

through a divorce, are substance abusers, have been sexually molested, have a severe social disorder or they are deeply in debt. They are so emotionally and financially obligated and self-emerged that they have nothing to offer. You might ask, "Who are you reaching?" We are reaching the average American!

An effective church must first perceive the needs of a society. It matters not how it should be. We must face the way it is and respond to those needs in a loving, relevant manner. Instead of criticizing those needs, we must then devise a plan to meet those needs. Sunday school was originally the product of the church being responsive and adaptable to the needs of society. When people did not know how to read, Sunday school was a place where they learned to read, while learning about God. The twentieth-century church has not been responsive to the needs of our generation. We have not molded our church programs to meet the needs. Instead we have clung to tradition. We have the same programs that the church began two hundred years ago, but we have them for the wrong reasons. We have them because they worked in the past. They no longer meet a relevant need of our society. Yet, they are what we know. So, we wait for the world to change so our program will work.

Immediately, when a new person comes into your church, the developing process should begin. Every program and every function should revolve around accomplishing the established Biblical commission, i.e., bringing each person to a saving knowledge of the Lord Jesus, developing a personal loving relationship with God, helping them to become whole through the love of God and launching them into a place of effective service. The numeric growth of the church is an outgrowth of the process, not the reason for the process!

It is our goal to have a person stable in about a year. For some it will take longer. Dysfunctional people do not change on our schedules. We must continually evaluate and modify all that we do in order to keep it effective and relevant. It takes time to overcome years of sexual, physical or emotional abuse. Our first objective is to help get them whole through a realization of the love of God, thus building a strong sense of Biblical self-worth. Until this is accomplished, nearly every loving effort will be falsely judged and misunderstood.

It is unlikely that a traditional paradigm of church

NOTES

will endure the changes necessary to actually meet the needs in today's society. It will take time to develop this awareness and willingness in your current congregation to move in this direction, but it can be done in a reasonable length of time. The church must be equipped to face the challenges of reaching the real world. They cannot be condemned for their present state. After all, they are where we led them.[3] They must be taken through a process. They do not realize their dysfunction. They will need to experience this very love that we are asking them to give to the world we are reaching.

When we honestly evaluated our church and the programs we offered, we realized that what had been very effective was no longer effective. We had to develop our leaders and congregation to think differently. We had to drop a service, add other functions and rethink nearly every area of ministry in order to become effective. After years of searching I found the key to developing the kind of leaders I wanted. For us, it involved less services with pulpit teaching and more development of people skills, more opportunities to model servant ministry and smaller groups where people processed what they were learning.

We found that the system that developed good disciples was the same system that would develop effective, loving leaders. We no longer had one system for developing the church and another for developing the leaders; it all happened at the same time. Promoting leaders was just a part of the continuum of developing a meaningful relationship with the Lord and becoming a disciple.

When a person comes to our church we seek to provide them with a sponsor. The sponsor is a person who comes into their home and shares some basic principles of being a believer.[4] The sponsor is trained by an Impact Group Leader who takes them out and models sponsoring a few times. Then the IGL[5] watches while they sponsor.

---

[3] The current condition of the world is in part due to the negative influence and failures of the church of the past.

[4] "*Relevant Ministry Workbook*," James B. Richards, Impact International Publications, Huntsville, Alabama

[5] IGL stands for Impact Group Leader. The IGL facilitates an Impact Group. Impact Groups have similarities to cell groups, fellowship groups, etc. However, there are some very essential differences. A handbook for Impact Group Leaders should be available from Impact International Publications by Summer 1999.

When they are comfortable, they are sent out with someone they will teach. Ideally, it will produce a never-ending cycle of converts, sponsor trainees, sponsors and IGLs.

The sponsor helps motivate the person to attend church, answers questions and basically befriends them for six weeks. If a relationship develops that is fine. By this time the new convert will be developing friendships of their own choice. It is at this time that the new convert is more in a relationship with the IGL. He has spent the previous six weeks attending an Impact Group. In this small, comfortable setting he has learned to open up and talk very freely. During the first six weeks the sponsor encourages the new convert to participate in four very important functions: 1) Church Membership Class 2) Soul Saving Sunday 3) Foundations of Faith Class 4) Discovery Class.[6]

The Church Membership Class is a one evening event that a person attends after attending four consecutive services and reads the book, *My Church My Family: How to Have a Healthy Relationship With the Church.*" In this class we help to diffuse false expectation. We provide a Church Member's Handbook that explains how our church functions. We use this time to clarify what we are offering as a church and what we are expecting from our members. The two main things we expect from our members are to give and to serve. We do not withhold any ministry from those who do not become members. We are simply asking them to make a meaningful commitment to serve the Lord Jesus together with us. For those who choose to join in our efforts to minister to our community they publicly express their intention to be an active member of our church in the following Sunday morning service.

The Foundations of Faith Class is a one-day event where the participants work through the foundational doctrines for Christian faith.[7] It is from these basic beliefs that we build every believer and every leader. It is not essential that everyone on our staff believe the same things. It is essential, however, that we all believe the same foundational doctrines. This class is essential in providing the doctrinal foundation for freedom from legalism and control. We want every member to live in freedom. We do

---

[6] These do not happen in any specific sequence. These different classes are offered regularly.

[7] *Foundations of the Faith Workbook*, James B. Richards, Impact International Publications, Huntsville, Alabama

not want them susceptible to manipulation, nor do we want any of our future leaders to have any inclinations toward domination as an acceptable form of leadership.

We have Soul Saving Sunday about four times a year. People put forth special effort to bring lost family and friends. The new believer may not be ready to win someone to Jesus, but are ready to bring them to church. Besides the many obvious benefits, this puts the new believer in the serving mode. He recognizes the need to serve through reaching out. Seeing a loved one come to Jesus can be a life-changing occurrence. It is often the beginning of a homogeneous social group that provides fellowship for the new convert and reaches a new segment of society.

The Discovery Class[8] is another special event where people are profiled to match their skills, gifts and passions to a specific place in the church where they are prepared to serve. We attempt to place people in an area they enjoy serving. Active participation has always been a successful area for us, primarily because we only place people where they enjoy serving. The idealistic concept that every parent should serve in children's church or that everyone has a particular place they should start and earn their way into a higher position tends to become very discouraging. Let people serve where they enjoy.

Ultimately, a person will find their way into leadership because they serve in an area for a period of time and demonstrate leadership skills. Because we do not esteem the leader above the worker we do not draw the codependent into the "leadership race." Our leadership slots are not filled with desperate people seeking approval. People do not neglect their families while seeking the approval of the pastors. Leadership is a not higher place of service; it is another place of service. It does not require better skills; it requires different skills.

Through this process it becomes self-evident who wants to serve and who wants attention. In this system we never promote a person on potential or friendship. We rarely turn away a potential leader because we are suspicious of their intentions. We seldom say, "no" to anyone. We show them the process. The process will prove them, one way or the other. When they see that all we offer is a place to serve, those with an agenda tend to move on to a system that is more conducive to codependent aspirations.

---

[8] The foundation for The Discovery Class is taken from the *Network* system developed by Bruce Bugbee, Don Cousins & Bill Hybels. Zondervan Publishing, Grand Rapids, Michigan

45

Questions for the heart:

1. Am I often disappointed with those I thought would be leaders?

2. Do my current leaders understand our community?

3. Do I have a plan in place to meet the needs of this generation?

4. Make an honest evaluation of your current programs:

   a. Are they meeting the real needs of the people?
   b. Do my programs allow people to get involved in ministry to others?
   c. Am I satisfied with the percentage of people serving?
   d. Do our converts get established in the foundational beliefs quickly?
      i. Do our new converts find a place to serve quickly?
      ii. Do I match people with their skill?
      iii. Do I put people in a place they will enjoy?

5. Do I have purpose for every program, or do I just have programs that tradition dictates?

6. Are our programs designed to meet the current needs in my community?

7. Is my organization flexible and adaptable as we recognize new needs?

7

COMMITMENT TO THE VISION

When we bring someone into our ministry team we are offering them an opportunity to serve together with us. We are bringing them along side to help us serve God's people by making them whole and equipping them for service.

By the time a person reaches the place of being approved for a staff position,[1] we often begin to assume they understand all that we desire and expect. It should be at this level that we take nothing for granted. The higher the level of responsibility, the greater the need for communication and clearly defined expectations.

By virtue of the fact that a person comes into our team, he/she is making a statement. They are saying they are willing to serve God's people. They are also saying that their vision can be fulfilled within the framework of our vision. They are saying that their desires are compatible and consistent with our desires. They are saying they accept our philosophy of ministry. They are also saying they accept ministry on our terms. All of this must be clearly established by more than mere verbal commitments. Through each step of the development it should be reaffirmed. Through relationships these issues are discussed throughout the entire developmental phase. Through meaningful leadership these commitments are modeled. These people have been observed and evaluated. There should be little room for doubt, but at this point there should be no assumptions.

As a person moves up the ladder in ministry, they do not gain new rights and privileges. Actually, they give up rights and privileges. They do so of there own free will, but it must happen. As leaders and workers we assume new levels of responsibility and commitment not privilege. We choose to live on a different plane than the people we serve. Far too many leaders have failed to walk this path. They are like a mutant cell on the body. They begin to

---

[1] All leaders should be considered staff. Never have volunteers. Have paid and non-paid staff. The requirements and expectations for all staff is the same. While respect should be given for the time limitations of the non-paid staff, the requirements should be the same.

reproduce other mutant cells until serious disease emerges. Likewise a selfish leader will raise up mutant followers who corrupt the entire body.

As a leader our morality and ethics must exemplify the gospel. We no longer live life from the shallow perspective of right and wrong. A responsible leader lives life from the perspective of influence and example. In 1 Corinthians 10:23, Paul said, *"All things are lawful for me, but all things are not expedient: all things are lawful for me, but all things edify not."* Paul's effect on others was more important than his personal freedom. It had to be considered more than mere right or wrong. He understood the role of the leader as an example. He willfully gave up many of his personal freedoms for the good of those he desired to help. One can never serve self and others. A caring leader can never exalt personal freedom above effective ministry.

This is what it means to be sanctified for the ministry. Positionally, we are all sanctified in Jesus. The word sanctified means "set apart." We are set apart unto God because we are in Christ. Yet, there is an act of sanctification that happens from the heart. This is the place where we set ourselves apart from things that hinder and destroy. This is where we give ourselves to Him for His people. Paul instructed Timothy about how to become a vessel of honor. *"But in a great house there are not only vessels of gold and of silver, but also of wood and of earth; and some to honour, and some to dishonour. If a man therefore purge himself from these, he shall be a vessel unto honour, sanctified, and meet for the master's use, and prepared unto every good work."* 1 Timothy 2:20-21. In this passage Paul tells Timothy to purge himself from vessels of dishonor in order to be "sanctified" for the Master's use.

The one who sanctifies himself for serving, no longer lives for self-gratification. We choose to live with a constant awareness of how we affect others. We not only sanctify ourselves unto the Lord, but we sanctify the Lord in our own hearts. We give the Lord and His work a special place in our heart. 1 Peter 3:15 says, *"But sanctify the Lord God in your hearts: and be ready always to give an answer to every man that asketh you a reason of the hope that is in you..."* As both Paul and Peter point out, it is this personal sanctification that makes us *ready*! The one who is always aware of their own desires notices everything that affects them. They live inward, subjective, self-centered lives. The one who is aware of others is sensitive to the needs of others and is ready to seize the opportunity to minister effectively to all.

Being selfless does not mean we have no value for ourselves. It is not a life of martyrdom or asceticism. Being selfless simply means that gratifying self is not the motivating factor in our life and ministry. We put God and His causes ahead of our causes. We do this as a matter of choice, because the love of God compels us. People who love God, love God's people. The apostle John said it this way, "*If a man says, I love God, and hateth his brother, he is a liar: for he that loveth not his brother whom he hath seen, how can he love God whom he hath not seen? And this commandment have we from him, That he who loveth God love his brother also.*" 1 John 4:20-21.

This standard must be taught and modeled by every leader in the organization. It is more than a method; it is a way of life. Then we must raise this as the standard for the type of people that will labor with us. We only want those who desire to serve. We only want those who are willing and desiring to live the life of sacrifice. We want a team of people around us who are willing to lay down their lives so others can be made whole and find a place of service. We are not making anyone do this. However, if they desire to be a part of our team this is the standard. Never violate this standard. You will always regret it in the end.

There is a paradox in leading and serving. We must lead those who become a part of our team. Leading is not controlling. We lead those who have made clearly defined commitments in order to bring safe, effective, organized ministry to the people. By becoming a part of our team, they have said and shown they will work our plan. We are not dominating them because we are leading them. We are simply coordinating the efforts of a team to accomplish greater things for God and His people.

There are many talented people who want to become a part of my team. Yet, what they want to do does not fit with what I am doing. Sometimes this is an opportunity for me to grow and expand my plan. Many times, however, for us to work together would result in chaos. This does not make them a bad person. They simply have a desire to lead a team of servants in a different direction. It would be wrong for me to bring this person onto my team and then attempt to change or control him.

More than once I have told talented people that they would be better suited doing their own thing or working with another ministry. I become supportive of them and have the opportunity of serving them as they launch out into their ministry and their vision. In every situation we have the opportunity to serve. It is our attempt to get every talented person on our team that gets us into control. When we have a team member whose vision does not work within ours, we are always moving in separate directions. Instead of supporting and developing their call, we hinder their call. They cannot serve us, nor can we serve them.

Many times a person who is a part of my team will begin to develop ministry concepts or passions that really do not work with what we are doing. I try to prayerfully determine if God is raising this person up to do his own thing, or if he simply has an attitude problem. So many times those who begin to go through these transitions are actually being developed by God to fulfill their call in a specific way. I must allow that person to develop. I must be ready to adapt and adopt, or I must be ready to launch them forth. Whatever I do, I must not become a hindrance to God working in someone's life.

Once again, this becomes an opportunity for me to launch this person out into their own vision. It would be wrong for me to control this person and force them to work my plan. Likewise, it would be wrong for them to come into my ministry and try to impose their plan on me. As the senior leader, we should give freedom to people. But they must give us that same freedom. We are not controlling a person because we ask them to work our plan. We are giving them the opportunity to determine if their vision can fit into our vision. But once they determine to become a part of our team it is their responsibility to fulfill their call in a way that is consistent with the organization.

When people do not want to work with us, we should let them go, for their benefit and ours. But we should be able to do this in a way that is not attacking or judgmental. People make choices, and they must live with the consequence of those choices. If you have clearly defined your ministry guidelines, and they have accepted them, they should abide by them or have the integrity to move along peaceably. For years our church would send out as many people into ministry as it would reach. Our numeric growth stayed the same, yet our cause grew around the world.

As the senior leader we should maintain an environment where people can develop into their own call without fear. Over the years I have sent out nearly every senior leader I have developed. Some of those people had the integrity to communicate with me about the changes in their heart. We walked it through together and I was able to bless them as they moved into another area of their call. Too often, bad experiences in the past made them afraid of honest communication. Many times they became dishonest and deceitful. Their lack of integrity brought about the negative situations they feared. Their lack of honesty and communication created conflict and chaos. But as I have modeled peaceful departure, those who have come up through this system are very comfortable expressing their desire for change. They have no fear of retribution or exclusion.

We must recruit, train and develop those who desire to be servants, not our servants, but servants of God and servants of God's people. Among servants there is rarely ever conflict. Servants are not working secret agendas. It is actually impossible to offend a servant. With a team of servants you can have productivity with peace. *"The blessing of the LORD, it maketh rich (prosperous, productive), and he addeth no sorrow (trouble, pain) with it."* Proverbs 10:22. By building a team of servants who can truly fulfill their personal vision within your organization, you can lead and not dominate. With every person striving toward the same goal, energy is not wasted attempting to keep everyone on track. There are no secret agendas and little chaos. The synergistic efforts of the team overcome inertia and keeps each team member empowered and encouraged to move ahead.

Questions for the heart:

1. Does my present system of developing people reaffirm servant-leadership at every step of development or do I assume the workers have a servant's heart because they are serving?

2. Does my leadership development make it clear that leaders give up privileges?

3. Can the vision of my leaders be fulfilled within the framework of my vision?

4. How do I insure that this happens?

5. Do I struggle when talented people want to do something that is not a part of my ministry?

   A. Do I try to change their plan?
   B. Do I feel there is something wrong with them if they   do not work my plan?
   C. Do I support them or exclude them when they walk in their own call?

6. Are my present leaders and I striving for the same goal?

7. When a staff member begins to feel the need to go in another direction does it often end in strife?

8. Does my staff feel the freedom to discuss the changes in their direction? Write some examples of when this has happened.

9. Do staff members usually leave on good terms or bad terms?

10. Make a list of the last ten people who were serving in some area and left. Beside their name, write "good" or "bad" to describe your present relationship with them.

SECTION 3

QUALIFICATIONS FOR EFFECTIVE LEADERS

Section three will begin to address the qualities of leaders and the process whereby we develop those qualities. It would be easy to become legalistic and pessimistic when we examine this aspect of the process. Too often any aspect of qualifications becomes polarized between extreme concepts of legalism and permissiveness. On the one hand we have the legalist who seeks to disqualify everyone and justify himself, or we have the permissive liberal who wants to overlook any aspect of qualification. The word "qualification" comes from the word "quality." Therefore, we must view the Biblical "qualification" more as "qualities." Qualities can be developed.

The Bible very clearly sets forth qualifications/ qualities for those who lead and serve God's people. The qualifications are not a matter of who is more righteous. It is a matter of who is more qualified. Who has the qualities to be most effective at leadership? We are all equally righteous in Jesus. Our personal failure cannot change our righteousness. Our righteousness is of Him, by Him and in Him. Yet, that does not mean we have the skills, qualities and strengths to lead and serve God's people in ways that will benefit their life.

Those who do not develop the qualities presented in God's qualifying lists will always be destroyers. They will not only destroy the people, they will destroy themselves. They may have good intentions, but God does have the final word in how we should view all of life's issues. Since it is His Kingdom, He has the only right to establish the qualifications, i.e. character strengths He desires in a servant-leader. We should abandon our foolish pride with its vain standards and accept His Word as the final and absolute authority.

We must open our hearts to develop a new paradigm. Rather than using this as a means of disqualifying and rejecting those who do not measure up, we must accept this as a commission of how we are to develop potential workers and leaders. Few lost people will walk into our churches with these qualities. It is our job to help them develop these qualities.

8

DEVELOPING SERVANTS

If we want different results, we will have to do things differently than we have done them before. Nearly everyone knows this simple saying, but few who quote it actually live it. Most of us would rather remain in the false sense of security that comes from doing things the way they have always been done. Tradition and culture provides a dichotomy. On the one hand we can feel safe, but we cannot accomplish our dreams. On the other, we launch into unlimited potential, but we face the fear of failure. Most people are stuck somewhere in this scenario. It is often easier to come up with flimsy excuses and blame-shifting than it is to move ahead in uncharted waters!

Even some of those who consider themselves to be pioneers are actually enslaved to a system of leadership that has not and will never work. Some who complain the loudest about what is not working are blindly following the same path as those they criticize. They may not be implementing the same practices, but they are making decisions based on the same principles. These decisions are continually producing the same frustrations. I had some friends who came out of a very control oriented ministerial organization. Their lives were shattered by the principles of leadership embraced by that organization. When this group recovered, they started new churches and launched out with new *methods* of leadership. Those new methods were based on the same principles of control, therefore they produced the same results. Different methods based on the same principles always produce the same results as the previous methods. It is not enough that we change our methods of ministry and leadership. We must change the principles and motives that propel and guide our actions. A quantum leap can only be taken when change is made at the smallest level. Therefore, change must happen at the level of principles and motives to produce a different kind of fruit. You may plant it at a different time of year. You may use a different kind of fertilizer. You may do everything different than before. But if you plant apple trees, you still get apples.

It is time we introduce new (not new from a Biblical perspective) concepts of leadership, team building, serving and training. It is time we seriously accept the standards of leadership as set forth in the Bible. We are not offering positions, titles or power. We are offering an opportunity to become servants in the Kingdom of God. All of our leadership development must come from this perspective.

In order to have a leadership team that is comprised of servants, all of our previous concepts must be challenged. The way we select leaders must change. We must consider qualifications other than those we have considered in the past. We must develop a new process of leadership training. We must be willing to develop people. It must go beyond methodology. We must be willing to model the role of a "servant leader." People must see the qualities in us that we desire to develop in them.

The church is ravaged by egocentric, self-centered, ambitious leaders seeking to build their own success, rather than that of the Kingdom of God. Love seems to motivate few of the actions and beliefs espoused by the American church. To often, the goal is not to use the ministry to serve the people, but to use the people to serve the ministry and the minister. The very selection of leaders and workers revolves around this warped concept. Too often the top criteria for selecting staff members and future leaders is blind loyalty to the current leaders. We have a deeply entrenched system of developing codependency and control. In some organizations those who are climbing the ladder polish shoes, mow lawns and wash cars. Their concept of servanthood says that when they get to the top, they will get some servants of their own. By the time a person in this system reaches "the top" their paradigm is so warped it is impossible to present them with Biblical values and standards. They want everyone to pay the price they paid.

The blindness of this mentality is the beginning of surrounding one's self with ineffective leaders and workers. When working from self-centered, egocentric motives we surround ourselves with people who are usually working their own agenda. They follow the self-centeredness they see modeled by the leader, and in the end they tear the church apart attempting to grasp their personal share of the flock. Self-centered leadership is the perfect breeding ground for those with self-centered motives. As I have traveled around the world for the last twenty years, I have

NOTES

55

found that most leaders feel a strong sense of betrayal. After going through hurt, frustration and loss, many have changed their methods. They are still, however, making decisions based on the same unbiblical principles. In the end the same unbiblical results prevail.

When we have truly committed ourselves to being servants of God's people, we will attract those who also desire to be servants. The person who is working a secret agenda will not desire to be a part of a team that holds no allure of glamour, position and power. In an environment of servant-leadership, it is very difficult to mask the hidden agendas of control and selfish ambition. When all we have to offer is the opportunity to serve, we will immediately weed out the undesirables. It may look as if we are weeding out many of the "good ones," but, trust me, you can afford to let them go. The truth is, you cannot afford to keep those who are not committed to serving God's people.

One of the starting places for getting on track is clearly stating your definition of success. What you consider success will ultimately determine the direction you will pursue. After you determine your definition of success, then identify someone you consider successful. That will tell you whom you will model. The seventies and eighties gave rise to many "mega-ministries." These ministries began to forge our current paradigm of success. Success became a matter of size, numbers and dollars. Every pastor in America was made to feel that his ministry was insignificant if it was not large, nationally known, and on television. In this blight of bright lights and glimmer we changed our target. It became acceptable to be "successful" at any price.[1] We lost sight of Jesus' commission to the church and to its leaders. It is no longer about bringing people into a meaningful relationship with the Lord. We lost value for effecting the quality of one's life. We began to see people as tools that we could use to fulfill our paradigm of success.

I have seen, first hand, the devastation of those who have sought the "new success." I have known super preachers who had nervous breakdowns. I have known those who were on drugs. I talked with one man who at

---

[1] I am in no way saying that all large churches are built on faulty principles. There are many large churches that are a blessing to millions. Do not try to figure out their motives, only your own.

one time had one of the largest ministries in America. He had women in every town. His lust for money was consuming. He was a habitual liar. His life was nothing but ego, sin and pain. Yet, every young preacher boy in that denomination looked to him as the model. He was a standard in his denomination by which to determine success. In the midst of this frenzy we made excuses for the improprieties of those leading these ministries. We overlooked the way they used people. The end began to justify the means. In order to have the success they defined, we started following their behavior. We accepted their principles, methods and, unfortunately, their lifestyle.

Now, many of those leaders have fallen. Millions of people have sacrificed financially. Thousands were cast by the wayside when they no longer had enough to give. The church has become a reproach to the nation, and we are still following the same path. We attempt to free ourselves from their pitfalls, yet, cling relentlessly to the faulty paradigm of success. We continue making decisions from the same principles, expecting different results.

The divisiveness among churches, ministries and Christians is the product of selfish, egocentric goals and principles. *"Only by pride cometh contention."* Proverbs 3:10. Through a desire to succeed, from a faulty paradigm of success, a man will be seeking his own success, not the goals of the Kingdom. Love, on the other hand, functions completely differently. 1 Corinthians 10:24 says, *"Let no man seek his own, but every man another's wealth."* 1 Corinthians 10:33 adds, *"Even as I please all men in all things, not seeking mine own profit, but the profit of many, that they may be saved."* It is so refreshing to meet the leader of a large church or ministry who never tried to be big. He/she just ministered to people and growth was the by-product.

I must redefine my concept of success to be consistent with Biblical principle. I must surrender my selfish ambition. I must organize in a way to work a more Biblically based plan. It is essential that I develop a staff that is committed to the role of servant-leadership. I need to be surrounded by talented, dedicated people who desire to be servants of God and His people. Together, my team and I must labor for the Kingdom of God.

As the senior leader, I must not only provide a clear definition of success; I must also model my definition. I must develop a system that demonstrates this definition for

NOTES

success and how it is achieved. I must do what few in the new church arena have done. I must develop leaders who are truly servants. Because this concept is so foreign, I must discover ways to continually reaffirm my definition of success. I must reward those who lead in this type of success. At this point we must rethink our understanding of the qualifications, the commission and the system of development and promotion.

I must make an unwavering commitment to live my life as a servant. I must follow the example of Jesus and establish a visible model for those who desire to be a part of my team. *"Let nothing be done through strife or vainglory, but in lowliness of mind let each esteem others better than themselves. Look not every man on his own things, but every man also on the things of others. Let this mind be in you, which was also in Christ Jesus, Who, being in the form of God, thought it not robbery to be equal with God, But made himself of no reputation, and took upon him the form of a servant..."* Philippians 2:3-7

Questions for the heart:

1. Am I using new methods based on destructive principles to develop my leaders?

2. Do my current leaders feel like a success when they affect a life or when they have public praise?

3. What is my definition of success?

4. Who do I consider successful?

5. If I fulfill my paradigm of success will it serve the people or me?

6. Are my personal freedoms more important to me than my ability to affect people?

7. Do I expect people to make special allowances for me since I am the pastor?

8. Do I tend to justify the actions of my leaders and myself?

9. If I continue along the same path what will be different about my leadership team? What will set us apart from every other similar organization?

10. Do I compare the size of my church to others?
    A. Does this affect my sense of success and failure?
    B. Am I embarrassed about the size of my organization?

11. Do I feel intimidated by those whose church is larger than mine?

9

QUALIFICATIONS FOR SERVING

Those who serve should usually make up the base from which we will develop those who lead. The process of development for serving should be a part of the system for developing leaders. As previously mentioned the entire ministry and all of its programs should be a continuum of one program. Thus, everyone is potentially in leadership training. They choose how far along the continuum they will travel. Additionally, there is no hierarchy of those who are accepted into special training programs. We are all on the same train, headed for the same destination. We can get off at any stop we choose.

As we look at the qualifications for those who would be deacons (servants), we could easily become discouraged by the lack of people who can fulfill these requirements. Traditionally, we have viewed this as a list of traits, which when absent, will disqualify the person from the opportunity of serving. I view this as a list of the traits that I desire to help develop in those who are committed to walking in discipleship unto the Lord. Titus gives many of these same traits as those which should be a part of the character list for godly men and women.[1] If a person desires to serve, those qualities become the standard for moral and ethical development.

Everyone who serves has influence. To some degree every Sunday School teacher, every person who sings in the worship team, every person who serves in any capacity is viewed as a leader. Their actions will affect people more than the actions of someone who is not involved. Therefore, we must develop those who serve in every area. Unfortunately, we have viewed the qualifications for deacons as something that only applies to those who hold an official office within the church. But a deacon is simply a servant. Therefore, this should be the goal for all who serve regardless of the capacity. Everyone who serves, whether he is a part of the five-fold ministry, one who carries food to the poor, or one who participates in the worship team, is a deacon or deaconess.[2]

---

[1] Titus 2:1-15

[2] The word "deacon" simply means servant.

When we bring people into our ministry team, whether paid or unpaid, full-time or part, whether leader or worker, we should use God's criterion for screening and for developing.

The qualifications for deacons and elders are character traits. They are not a list of qualifications wherein failure on any one point would be grounds for disqualification from serving. These are character traits that we must look for in those who become a part of our team. Their character in these areas will determine their character in serving. Because the church has misunderstood the concept being presented in this list of qualities, we have elevated some qualifications above the others. Because we have failed to see God's wisdom in each of these virtues, we have eliminated some altogether, thus we have filled our positions with corrupt, ineffective people. Furthermore, since these are God's qualifying factors we should evaluate our developmental process to determine if we are actually encouraging and developing these traits. If not, we should revise our process.

The following is a Biblical list of qualities we desire to develop in those who express the desire to serve:[3]

GRAVE

As much as anything, the word "grave" speaks of honor, integrity and honesty. This is a general trait, yet, if people have no honor, we cannot entrust them with God's people. More than once in more than twenty-five years of ministry, I have promoted a person to a place of honor only to discover that he/she was not a person of honor. Honor is the sum total of personal esteem with which we view ourselves and conduct our lives. People of honor recognize they are a new creation in Christ. They have an internal sense of dignity, worth and righteousness. From that sense of honor, all of their affairs are conducted with honor.

When a person who has no honor is found in a place of honor, they will always misuse that position.

---

[3] In 1 Timothy 3:11, the word "wives" probably applies to deaconesses; therefore, qualities for deaconesses are included in this list.

They will use it as a place to meet their needs instead of the needs of the people. In the chapter entitled "Giving Honor," we will discuss the perversion of honor that is presently promoted in the church world. None of us would ever deliberately promote a dishonest person into leadership. Yet, we do it regularly. The dishonesty is seldom a blatant intent to do wrong. It is usually the result of a person who has no personal sense of honor acting out of their unbiblical sense of honor and identity. If you believe you are righteous and you feel righteous, it is hard to act unrighteous. If you feel like a part of the body of Christ, it is hard to dishonor the body.

Proverbs 26:1 says, "*As snow in summer, and as rain in harvest, so honor is not seemly for a fool.*" A foolish person brings dishonor to what should be a place of honor. In years gone by there has been inordinate pressure placed on the congregation to honor the offices in the church. Honor cannot be forced. A person gives honor from their heart. When honor is not given to an office, either the person is incapable of giving honor, or the person in the office is not worthy of honor. To solicit honor is a breach of all that honor contains.

We must look at honesty in the little areas of life. A person of honor will have integrity in every area of life. Not just the "big things." They do what they say, when they say, how they say. They do not leave people in a bind when it is inconvenient for them. As it says in Psalms 15:4 about the righteous, "*He sweareth to his own hurt and changeth not.*" A grave person realizes the importance of his/her personal testimony. They do not take the things of God lightly. They know their behavior is always affecting others. They realize that their life is the only Bible that some will ever read.

One of the key factors that identifies a person of honor is that he is able to give honor. They have respect for their team members. They know that others are counting on them. They understand that their performance effects the performance of the entire team. They see how their part of the task is essential to the big picture. Therefore, they consider no part small or unimportant. When they are late they hold up the entire team. Yes, even something as small as punctuality has meaning in light of its effect on the other team members. Punctuality is a part of honesty and respect. People who are consistently late do not have respect for their task, their position or the other team members. They do not understand how their part effects the whole.

Being a servant of God is an honorable task. A grave person accepts the task and brings honor to the position. He/she does not expect the position to bring them honor.

NOT DOUBLE-TONGUED

Double-tongued means exactly how it sounds. It is the issue of honesty and deceit. Strong's[4] says that to be double-tongued is to tell different stories. The double-tongued person is not accurate in their account of things. They change their stories. Once again, this is seldom the result of a blatant desire to deceive. This is a reflection of a person who has a need for approval. Or, this could be a self-centered person who only allows subjective evaluation.

The people who serve with us become our five senses. We depend on them to present accurate information to us and to the people. We need their input to make decisions. Inaccurate input will cause inaccurate decisions. No decision is any better than the information upon which it is based. No information is any more accurate than the character and perception of the person presenting it.

Many double-tongued people are not outright liars. Many times they have a tendency to evaluate situations and pass on their evaluation rather than the actual account. They assume their interpretation to be reality. Often they do not differentiate between what happened and how it made them feel. Or, they may simply over emphasize one aspect of the facts. As the senior leader, we need to make the evaluation. What we need from people are the facts, not their evaluation of the facts. It is good to get the facts and then allow the person who observed the event to give their evaluation, but we must always know which is which. Failure to repeat the facts accurately is lying. The double-tongued person often desires to influence the view of the leader. They want the leader to have the same evaluation as them, thus influencing the outcome.

---

[4] Logos Bible Software, Logos Research Systems, Inc., Oak Harbor, Washington

The double-tongued person will misrepresent you to the people. They will evaluate your statements and actions. They will pass judgement on you, and they will attempt to make others have that same judgement. They will control how others see you. For example, A member of a team does something improperly. You tell the team leader they should meet with their team and make sure it happens in an appropriate manner. Instead, they meet with the team and say, "The pastor is really mad. He said that this better never happen again." This personal slant on the truth causes people to view you in a very negative light. Because it is a partial truth, there are times that your actions will seem to verify the statement. This person just assassinated you as a way to preserve their position with their team.

A double-tongued person is worse than an outright liar. An outright liar is easy to refute. Many of the things they lie about never even happened. But a double-tongued person is talking about something that actually happened. So many of their statements are true and verifiable that it makes their story believable. The worst damage that has ever occurred in my church was the work of one double-tongued girl who was here for several years. She was not a leader, but she was close enough to me that she had a degree of credibility. She never outright lied about any-thing. She simply repeated statements that she heard with a slant on them. She hurt more people than the most vicious gossips and liars had ever done.

NOT GIVEN TO MUCH WINE

I wish this had been left out of the Bible. Like it or not this is not making the issue of drinking absolutely forbidden. Many people use this to their own destruction. But we can use this in a positive way to understand the character of a person.

I have never been adamantly against a person for drinking. The Bible does not give me the right to do that. It does, however, tell me that a person given to much wine is not a candidate to be a servant with me. A person given to much wine would be more than a person who gets drunk. It would be a person that was without discretion in the way he handles himself. An honorable person recognizes his influence over others. If he chooses to partake of alcohol it would be in a setting that was befitting of a person with character. There would be consideration for the setting and for those present. A person who fails to have this discretion is a person who cannot be trusted with God's people. He is more interested in fulfilling personal freedom and personal passion than maintaining effectiveness with the people.

In Bible times wine was a part of the daily drink. There was no social stigma about a person drinking wine. It was, however, condemned to drink too much wine. In America, we have no need to drink wine. One can buy non-alcoholic beer and wine that would satisfy the taste for one so inclined. A Connoisseur of wine may desire a specific wine with a meal. But all in all, drinking in America has one purpose: intoxication. Regardless of the innocence, drinking is very damaging to one's personal testimony *in this culture*.[5]

When I ponder on this verse I expand it to any kind of substance abuse, including food. Please note that I did not say, "including overweight people." Not every overweight person is a glutton. I have known very few overweight people whose problem was simply a lack of control.

People who tend to abuse any type of substance are not people that I will quickly trust. Substance abuse represents a life that is out of control. Self-control is essential for servants. Proverbs 25:28 describes the person without self-control. *"He that hath no rule over his own spirit is like a city that is broken down, and without walls."* A person who can control their appetites will be able to maintain character in pressure situations, tempting situations, emotional situations...in nearly any situation. I do not want to depend on people who will blow out in a pressure situation. Substance abuse is a continuum of codependency.[6] Codependency is that tendency to look outside of God in our own heart for pleasure, fulfillment or self-worth. This tendency to search for fulfillment outside

---

[5] In some cultures drinking is a very acceptable part of life. In parts of Europe the leaders and the church will drink beer and talk about God after the service, yet, they would never drink caffeine. A caring leader considers the culture and the conscience of the people involved without becoming bound himself.

[6] *"Escape From Codependent Christianity,"* James B. Richards, Impact International Publications, Huntsville, Alabama

of oneself can lead to many personal weaknesses. As someone has said, "Codependency is the mother of all addictions." This person will ultimately use the people and their position as a source of personal gratification.

It is my desire to develop wholeness, satisfaction and contentment in our people so they have no need of giving themselves to any extreme. A discontented person will fall prey to their craving for food, alcohol, sex, popularity or power at the expense of God's people.

NOT GREEDY OF FILTHY LUCRE

This phrase talks about someone who is eager for gain. We all have the need and the desire to prosper and succeed. There is nothing wrong with that desire. I personally believe the desire to succeed is God-given. There is, however, a point in being eager for gain where one will compromise the good of the people. We cannot be in the ministry for ourselves. We must be there to serve. A true servant will serve whether he is paid or non-paid. It is not the position that counts; it is the desire to serve.

While it is good and scriptural for a person to be paid from the fruit of their labor, that point has been very exaggerated in recent years. There was a time when ministers were kept on starvation standards, in the name of the Lord. Deacons unscripturally held the purse strings of the minister. In recent years the pendulum seems to have swung too far in the other direction. Every preacher thinks the church owes him/her a living. So much so, that many people will not serve if they are not paid. This is not an individual that can be trusted. This is not someone who should have influence with God's people.

God never called us Christians. God called us believers, disciples and stewards. All of these words indicate commitment and personal responsibility. A steward is one who manages their life and resources for the Kingdom of God. A servant of the Lord understands that he/she has been bought. Our life is not our own. We belong to the Lord. The steward desires to see others experience God. The steward recognizes their place of service and does it expecting no reward or compensation. The steward never claims personal ownership. He acknowledges that all he is and all he has belongs to the Lord. He is simply managing his life and resources for the Lord.

In applying this qualification, however, we must look at the person's life as a whole. Does this person pursue "base gain, filthy lucre" in their personal life and business? If so, they are not yet a candidate for one who should be trusted to serve in certain areas.[7] They will be tempted to pervert and exploit their position.

I have made an interesting observation in this area. I have seen people that would be dependable on their jobs to do certain things. But, when asked to do those same things in an area of ministry, they were undependable. This shows me they are motivated by money more than they are motivated by the desire to serve. Many times I have tried to justify this type of behavior. After all, I reasoned, they do not have as much time to do this as needed, etc. But every time I trusted a person with this behavior it ended in disaster. In most cases these people eventually backslid.

HOLDING THE MYSTERY OF THE FAITH IN A PURE CONSCIENCE

This directive stands in opposition to the previous three. The previous three speak of one who is not grave, serious and dignified. Only when one holds the mystery of the faith in a pure conscience will he be free from the previous pitfalls. Holding the mystery of the faith in a pure conscience exceeds far beyond how he serves in his ministry. It has to do with the way he handles his life and commitment to Christ.

I want to be surrounded by those who have honor for their own conscience. If a man will defile his own conscience, he will have little concern for the conscience of others. One who is sensitive to his own conscience represents one who is sensitive and listening. This person can be trusted in the absence of personal oversight. When he does not know exactly what to do, he will always consider his conscience and the conscience of the people.

---

[7] It is important to match a person's character to the place they seek to serve. As character is developed other areas of service can be explored.

When one, in the name of freedom, leads a believer to defile his own conscience, he is a destroyer.

FIRST LET THEM BE PROVED

This is one of the most essential keys to success. Before one is entrusted with the care of God's people they must be proved. The enhanced Strong's Lexicon[8] defines this word "proved" as, "to test, examine, prove, scrutinize (to see whether a thing is genuine or not), as metals to recognize as genuine after examination, to approve, deem worthy."

One of the greatest mistakes made in the process of promotion is to promote[9] a person on the basis of potential. A person's potential is no indicator of their future performance. Too often we find ourselves standing on a foot out of joint, because we did not prove the faithfulness of those on whom we depend. Proverbs 25:19 says, *"Confidence in an unfaithful man in time of trouble is like a broken tooth, and a foot out of joint."* When we find ourselves often depending on an unfaithful person, we must realize that we are the foolish ones. Our system of personal development must have the essential elements for proving faithfulness, skill and the previously mentioned character traits.

Character is proved one step at a time. There is no one test that will prove the quality of a man's character and commitment. A person may be faithful in an area of his liking, but totally undependable in another. For this reason, every person must be walked through the developmental process. To assume one's character automatically puts us in a position to violate the admonition to prove before trusting. It is actually judging. God does not give us the right to judge the character of another. He does tell us to observe and when the fruit grows, we know the person.

NOT SLANDERERS

A leader cannot be one who slanders and criticizes those he/she serves or the team with whom they serve. Proverbs 10:18 says that a slanderer is a fool. A slanderer

---

[8] Ibid.

[9] Remember that promotion is simply the next step in serving. It is not a step up. It is a step of more trust and responsibility.

finds no worth for the people. One cannot serve those for whom they have no value or worth. A slanderer distorts the view of those to whom they speak. They corrupt compassion and rob mercy from the hearts of those who desire to serve and minister.

Love overlooks faults, it does not justify them, it over looks them. We want those who serve to look for the best in others. From those who serve will emerge those who will lead. A leader cannot be a slanderer. One cannot serve and destroy simultaneously. A slanderer is always working an agenda. However innocent it may seem, a person slanders for a reason. That reason must be resolved before that person can be entrusted with the lives of God's people.

SOBER

The Bible speaks of being sober-minded. One who is sober minded is one who thinks clearly and rationally. The primary factor for being sober is derived from not being drunk on the lust for things of the world. A person can become intoxicated on many things. He can be drunk with power, the lust of the flesh, the pride of life, the need to succeed, or any obsessive desire.

When one becomes intoxicated they become un-aware of their environment; their view becomes distorted. In this drunken condition they can give themselves to any strange lust. Those who serve cannot be obsessive. The fulfillment of their obsession will supercede the purposes of God and the purposes of the ministry. His perception must not be clouded by a drunken state of obsession. He must always see things from a sober mind.

FAITHFUL IN ALL THINGS

In the end, what we want is faithfulness, i.e. faithfulness to God, faithfulness to the people and faithfulness to the objectives of the organization. Those who walk worthy of the ministry are faithful. It is not suggested that a steward be faithful; it is required. *"Moreover it is required in stewards, that a man be found faithful."* 1 Corinthians 4:2.

The Greek words for "believe" and "obey" are

synonymous. There is really no such thing as believing and not obeying. Unfortunately, obeying does not always equate believing. There is much obedience that comes from fear and legalism. Likewise, true faithfulness is always a heart issue. It springs from a heart of belief, trust and love. We do not want those who are merely obedient, compliant and controllable. We want those who serve out of a sense of sonship, love, appreciation and honor. We do not need to develop a false system of judgement to determine who is genuine. We must simply be willing to observe over a long period of time, and the truth will emerge. The person with a secret agenda will never endure the process of becoming a servant. Or, better yet, they will grow to see the plan of God and surrender their life in a new way to the Lordship of Jesus.

I do not expect every person to be blameless on every point. I do, however, use this list as a way to evaluate the general character of those who desire to become servants. Additionally, I use this list to evaluate the effectiveness of the programs we develop. I do not expect the people I reach to have many, if any, of these qualities. But I do expect them to grow in these areas. If not, then I must reevaluate the ministry I am offering and make the necessary adjustments.

Questions for the heart:

Use the following questions as a guide to help you evaluate your process of developing servants.

1. Do I put more emphasis on serving than on developing the character of a servant?

2. Do I over emphasize certain traits while ignoring other traits?

3. Make a list of each of the traits listed and ask the following question: Is our present program developing these traits in our people?

4. List each trait and determine how and where this is being developed?

5. Is there any one trait that seems to be lacking in our people? Which ones.

6. What can I do to develop this quality in our people.

7. Meet with your staff and allow them to discuss and evaluate your current success at developing these qualities in the people.

10

QUALIFICATIONS FOR LEADERS

The Bible is full of important traits for the effective leader. We will not address every Biblical qualification, nor will we explain those we list in complete detail. The qualifications used here are taken from listings in the New Testament books of Timothy and Titus. It is essential to remind ourselves that this is not a list of things that will disqualify a person. If this were the case, no one would be qualified for leadership. If we use this as a checklist, giving each trait equal value, we will never find anyone who measures up.

These traits represent a character sketch rather than a checklist. This will draw a picture of the "kind" of person who will be effective in leadership. Too often we think of these characteristics solely as a list of qualifications and tend to miss their higher value. Not only do these traits help us understand the character sketch of the leader, they show us the traits needed to be an effective leader. Those who lack these traits may be dynamic in isolated areas, but they will fail in many.

We must not look at this list at the beginning of our ministry and never consider it again until we have failed at one of the points. We need to use this list of qualities as a compass to keep us on course. We should continually cultivate these traits in our life. These should be constant reminders of the character required to remain effective. These character traits become a lifestyle that will keep us on target. When these traits disappear from our lives, they are replaced with opposing, destructive traits. These self-centered traits creep in and steal our effectiveness, thereby disqualifying us from leadership at that point in time.

As mentioned previously, this gives us a target for understanding how we should develop leaders. These are traits that should be developed in every life. These are a part of the continuum of personal development. If we know the target for developing our leaders we can look at how we are developing people to determine the congruency of our efforts.

No one will fully possess all of these traits. We may have them all in different measure. There will be times when we are stronger in one than another. But this is a character sketch to which we should dedicate our life. Likewise, these are the qualities that our leadership training process should develop.

BLAMELESS

The first trait, "blameless," if taken literally, would disqualify us all. The concept of being blameless comes from the translation of a compound word which combines the meanings of, "take hold, upon and not." [1] The traditional concept of blameless would come from the concept of "one who could not be taken hold of" through accusation or character flaw. While the literal meaning is fully acceptable, there is great latitude for other views. When the original language lends itself to several possible translations, it is essential that we incorporate the full scope of meaning into our understanding.

The phrase, "not take hold upon" could also refer to the non-aggressive attempt to take the ministry by force. Too many times, the very qualifications presented by Jesus are totally ignored in leadership development.[2] His insistence that we could not rule over one another, nor exercise authority over one another, is not only denied, but the very opposite is encouraged.[3]

In many circles, the teaching of spiritual authority is the cornerstone for developing church members and church leaders. The entire hierarchy is built around the premise that the people should submit to and obey the leaders without question. Serving the system and the leaders is emphasized more than the cause and the people. Leaders become the power brokers, and members become the commodities. This emphasizes the issue of power over the issue of serving.

---

[1] *Word Studies in the Greek New Testament*, Kenneth S. Wuest, Eerdman's Publishing Company, Grand Rapid, Michigan

[2] Mark 10:42-45, "*But Jesus called them* to him, *and saith unto them, Ye know that they which are accounted to rule over the Gentiles exercise lordship over them; and their great ones exercise authority upon them.* [43]*But so shall it not be among you: but whosoever will be great among you, shall be your minister:* [44]*And whosoever of you will be the chiefest, shall be servant of all.* [45]*For even the Son of man came not to be ministered unto, but to minister, and to give his life a ransom for many.*"

[3] "*Leadership That Builds People, Volume I,*" James B. Richards, Impact International Publications, Huntsville, Alabama

73

In this environment, the power-hungry gravitate toward leadership positions. It becomes something at which they grasp. It becomes a place to feed the ego rather than feed the sheep. They try to take it forcibly. When the Bible says, "*The violent take the Kingdom by force,*" it is not a recommendation as much as it is a criticism. The violent natured view leadership, faith and power in the Kingdom of God as something that can be forcibly taken, thereby denying all that Jesus taught and modeled.

There is yet another essential aspect to the concept, "not take hold upon." When a leader has weaknesses in the following areas, these become places where he can be taken. One of the words for demon possessed literally means "taken." We lose control of our life when we are taken, vexed and obsessed.

Developing these character traits not only protects the congregation, it protects the leader. When a person falls, it will be because he is *taken* in one of these areas where he has not developed his personal character.

THE HUSBAND OF ONE WIFE[4]

Too often a person manages to stay married, but their personal life style denies the very heart of marriage. I recall an interesting situation in a particular denomination. There were two men in a particular church. One man was divorced because his wife had been unfaithful and had abandoned him and his children. While this man was a faithful father and husband, he had been denied the opportunity to fulfill his call because he was divorced. In the same church, there was a man who had committed adultery more than once, yet his wife stayed with him. He was allowed to serve and be ordained. He had never been divorced. His wife, who had endured much, chose to forgive her husband.

This gross negligence of interpretation put one man in the ministry and one man out of the ministry. The way this verse was misused twisted it into a checklist that rewarded the wicked and punished the righteous.[5] Its

---

[4] The use of the male gender is used to remain consistent with the way the passage is written. It is in no way meant to exclude women from leadership roles. The same character traits apply to both men and women.

[5] Proverbs 17:15, "*He that justifieth the wicked, and he that condemneth the just, even they both* are *abomination to the LORD.*"

74

misuse measured the character of the wife not the man. Based on the character of the wife, a disqualified man was given a position; a qualified man was denied a position. This is a qualification where we too often miss the higher value.

This verse has been stretched and pulled in every conceivable direction; but at the heart of this passage we see, once again, this is a reference to the character or nature of the man. A.T. Robertson,[6] Kenneth Wuest[7] and others agree that this passage refers to monogamy. This person cannot be a polygamist. Literally translated, it means "one wife at a time." Yet, this literal translation misses the point. Kenneth Wuest translates this trait as "a one woman sort of man." This seems to capture the essence of the passage more effectively than any translation I have seen.

A "one-woman sort of man" brings an image to mind that supercedes whether the person has been married or divorced. It addresses the character of the person. It delves into the way one conducts oneself. This phrase speaks of the faithfulness, loyalty and dedication of a person. There are many who have never gone through a divorce, yet they are not a "one-woman sort of man." In my mind this even supercedes whether the person has committed adultery. Many who are faithful in deed are not faithful in heart.

I want my leaders to be committed to their spouse. I know that a person will ultimately treat the church the way he treats his family. He may use different tactics, but his motives will be the same. I do not just want him married to one person; I want him to be the kind of person who endears himself to his spouse. A one-woman sort of man does not have a wandering eye. This is a person who can accept the responsibility that comes with the high level of trust given to the minister. The minister deals with confidential information. He/she is exposed to the weaknesses and vulnerabilities of the congregation. A "one-woman sort of man" will not exploit others for personal gratification or gain. It is not easy for him to "be taken" in this area.

More than whether a person has or has not been divorced, we need to develop the kind of character that

---

[6] "*Word Pictures in the New Testament*," A.T. Robertson, Broadman Press, Nashville, Tennessee

[7] Ibid.

makes him a "one-woman sort of man." Regardless of his past, time will reveal this trait. Most of the people I reach have had multiple marriages. I have had members of my church that have been married as many as eight times. I have often seen those with a checkered past become very faithful, dedicated mates whose character exceeded the legalistic interpretation of this passage.

VIGILANT

Vigilant, according to every reliable source, should be translated "temperate." Most are quick to reduce this to the concept of "temperate in consuming alcoholic beverages." While this is, no doubt, a worthy trait for a leader, we must once again look to the larger picture of the character sketch. The issue of alcoholic drink has been clearly addressed. It is doubtful this is a repetitive reference to this issue.

A leader should be temperate or moderate in every area of life. Moderation is an essential quality for peace and fulfillment. He who wants too much, takes too much! Temptation does not begin with the devil; it begins with our desires. Excessive desire will ultimately turn one's head in the direction of excessive behavior. When the opportunity is presented, the one who is not temperate will be drawn into destruction by his own desire.[8] The leader should be moderate in finances, theology and lifestyle. He must not be ruled by excess, including temper. Wuest and others point out that he must be self-controlled. He cannot be given to a violent temper.

A moderate man will not give himself to every "spiritual fad." He will not be looking for the "magic bullet" theological answer that will solve every problem. He will not create instability through the pursuit of teachings that tickle the ears and boost his ego. The temperate will not swing from one theological position to another. When changes of position become necessary, he/she will bring about the appropriate change through moderate, productive means.

The impulsive, immature leader creates an environment and urgency that stimulates fear and uncertainty. He throws away the validity of past beliefs, thereby undermin-

---

[8] James 1:14 *"But every man is tempted, when he is drawn away of his own lust, and enticed."*

76

ing all beliefs.

A temperate person is one who does not easily become addicted. This leader does not allow himself to become vexed by the desires of the world. He/she is not using possessions, acknowledgements and other vanities as a source of fulfillment. Moderation is a way of life in every area.

SOBER

Sober would probably better refer to sober-minded. The sober-minded will think clearly. His judgement will not be clouded with obsessive desires. Because he is sober-minded, he will understand the priorities of leadership.

One important characteristic of a leader is that he never loses sight of the destination. He always holds the big picture clear in his mind. Thus, he does not become sidetracked by other issues. Because the clear-minded leader always has the goal in mind, he never leads people astray.

Too often the church is led astray. If they were, in fact, led into sin it would be easy to identify and correct. The twentieth-century church seems to continually be sidetracked by non-essential issues that lead the church into non-productivity and false spirituality. We tend to major on the minors. It is not wrong per se; it is simply over emphasized until the Biblical destination is lost.

To be a success in today's "Christian market," one must specialize. We are expected to find one thing that establishes a reputation and exploit it. People put us under pressure to produce and then reproduce. We succumb to the pressure. It becomes the only thing that will keep people coming to our meetings. It is our "claim to fame." I have seen so many people caught in this trap. I have had certain ministers confide that if certain things did not happen in their services the people would stop coming. Success will always intoxicate the foolish of heart. *"For the turning away of the simple shall slay them, and the prosperity of fools shall destroy them."* Proverbs 1:32.

Refusal to duplicate caused Jesus to experience very erratic attendance in His meetings. He refused to build His ministry around the expectations of the people. He never specialized. He was clear-minded. He understood and stuck to the mission. Yet, many came with their own agenda attempting to force Him into reproducing. *"Jesus answered them and said, Verily, verily, I say unto you, Ye seek me, not because ye saw the miracles, but because ye did eat of the loaves, and were filled."* John 6:26.

Our mission statement should provide us with the goal to which we are committed. If we remain sober, we will relentlessly lead the people in that direction. A leader cannot be one who is easily intoxicated with fads, results or ego. He/she must maintain a clear mind with a clear-cut Biblical agenda.

OF GOOD BEHAVIOR

This is a term that has a broad meaning. *"The Expositor's Bible Commentary"*[9] does an excellent job of presenting this character trait as respectable, honorable and orderly. Once again, we find the fuller meaning in a character concept instead of a single qualifying trait. The word "orderly" seems to be the concept that governs the realization of this word. An honorable person knows how to order his/her life in an acceptable manner. He/she recognizes the value of living a respectable life and has the means to order his/her life accordingly.

In recent years, there has been excessive teaching about showing honor to those in the ministry. While this is no doubt a need that exists in the body of Christ, it is perversion of honor. We should walk in honor and treat others with honor. Jesus never demanded that anyone give Him a certain level of respect, honor or special treatment. When we demand how others should treat us, it is no longer our honor, but theirs. We should live a life of honor and let people respond to us the way their character dictates. We should model the giving of honor.

Paul maintained his honor. He stated in 1 Corinthians 6:12, *"All things are lawful unto me, but all things are not expedient: all things are lawful for me, but I will not be brought under the power of any."* Paul did not order his life on the basis of what was legally or spiritually acceptable. He did not do something simply because he could. He did not turn freedom into excess or obligation. He valued the influence that came by living an orderly, responsible life. Likewise, he realized the traps that lay

---

[9] *The Expositor's Bible Commentary Volume 11*, Zondervan Publishing House, Grand Rapids, Michigan

ahead for those who indulged in self-gratification.

The self-serving leader justifies unacceptable behavior under the cloak of freedom. Too often, freedom becomes the destruction of the leader and those who follow. As both Peter and Paul remind us, freedom has responsibility. *"As free, and not using your liberty for a cloke of maliciousness, but as the servants of God."* 1 Peter 2:16. *"While they promise them liberty, they themselves are the servants of corruption: for of whom a man is overcome, of the same is he brought in bondage."* 2 Peter 2:19. Love and wisdom should govern our actions. *"For, brethren, ye have been called unto liberty; only use not liberty for an occasion to the flesh, but by love serve one another."* Galatians 5:13. Freedom empowers us to love the unlovable, not to live in excess.

"Orderly" points out another important trait. An orderly person is one who is organized. It takes a high level of personal organization to be an effective leader. How one manages time, resources and personal relationships will always affect the quality of ministry offered to others. Chaos in one's personal life distracts from the responsibilities of leadership.

GIVEN TO HOSPITALITY

The very concept of hospitality contradicts the modern concept of the successful, mega-minister. It seems the more successful one becomes, the more estranged they become from the very people they are called to serve. Obviously, there are demands on the minister of a large organization. He can, in no way, live up to the expectations of all the people. Even Jesus devoted His major personal ministry to twelve, sometimes enlarging his scope to the 70 or 120. Yet, He never lost that personal touch. He was never estranged from the people. Growth demands that we focus our attention on the leaders we are developing. We serve and develop them as they serve the people. This is an acceptable and essential pattern. Yet, hospitality should still be an earmark of the leader, not isolation.

One should make every attempt to be as approachable and accessible as possible. Isolation is the breeding ground for all manner of strange ideas. The demoniac, the obsessed and the defeated seek isolation as a cloak to cover their defeated lifestyle. In isolation everything seems normal. It is only in the proving ground of open relation-

NOTES

79

ships that we discover the validity and the application of our beliefs.

A person can wear a mask in every arena of life. The only place one sees the real person is in the home. The pedophile, the abuser and the controller seek extreme isolation. The home is the place where he has created the illusion that excessive behavior is normal. When we know someone at home, we know him. While some are more given to hospitality than others, this trait must be developed in the effective leader.

Several reliable sources translate the term "given to hospitality" as "loving strangers." The concept of hospitality and loving strangers comes from the conditions at the time of this writing, where Christians depended upon the hospitality of others to provide lodging and food during travel. This is, once again, a character sketch of the person who is loving, open and welcomes others into his/her home.

APT TO TEACH

Lenski translates "apt to teach" as "willing to teach."[10] This is not the person who is always giving advice. The Greek word points to didactic instruction. The ability to give meaningful instruction has, as a prerequisite, the previously mentioned character traits. This will be a person whose instruction proceeds from the kind of character that models the meaning of the instruction. This is not the voice of the "know it all," or, the one who says, but does not do.

1 Timothy 1:5 says, "*Now the end of the commandment is charity out of a pure heart, and of a good conscience, and of faith unfeigned.*" The responsible teacher does not make the passing of information the goal of teaching, nor does he make the impartation of secret knowledge and new revelation the goal of teaching. The goal of the responsible teacher is to develop people in love from a pure heart and establish people in those things that will facilitate a good conscience and faith.

The responsible teacher does not teach to "get people right." To teach from that perspective would be

---

[10] *The Interpretation of St. Paul's Epistles to the Colossians, to the Thessalonians, to Timothy, to Titus and to Philemon*, R.C.H. Lenski, Augsburg Publishing House, Minneapolis, Minnesota

quite destructive. It possesses the essential premise that they are wrong and we are right. The Apostle John said, "*I have not written unto you because you know not the truth, but because ye know it.*" He saw his role as one who confirms truth. He believed God spoke to people. He believed that people would recognize the Word of God because it would confirm what was in their heart. He wrote this in sharp contrast to those who insisted that the convert lacked something from God that could only be obtained through the insight and anointing of the teacher/preacher.

The mature teacher knows that righteousness came into man when he received Jesus. The role of the teacher is to develop people's faith to believe and be empowered in faith-righteousness, thus confirming the finished work of the Lord. He does not add to it as if there is something lacking. To add to the finished work is to deny it. The wise teacher compels the believer to look into his own heart, to read and believe the Bible, to walk with the Spirit and thereby experience completeness in Jesus.

"*The Expositor's Bible Commentary*"[11] quotes Vine as saying, "Not merely a readiness to teach is implied, but the spiritual power to do so as the outcome of prayerful meditation in the Word of God and the practical application of its truth."

NOT GIVEN TO WINE

This was adequately covered in Section three, Chapter nine, entitled "*Qualifications for Serving.*"

NO STRIKER

All sources agree that, "not a striker" is a character sketch that stands opposed to one who is ready to respond with a fight. This trait describes the one who is not quick-tempered. A quick-tempered individual is bound in pride. Anger is the violent response to one's fragile self-worth being violated. Because this person is not committed to being a peacemaker, he destroys those who are perceived as a threat.

No doubt, this literally refers to one who responds

---

[11] *The Expositor's Bible Commentary Volume 11*, Zondervan Publishing House, Grand Rapids, Michigan

with physical violence. However, I personally feel it refers to one who tends to respond with any aggressive behavior. The one who argues and defends must first have many other character flaws that are unacceptable for the effective leader. Self-centered is the main word that comes to mind.

When one is self-centered, everything is about them. It is about how they look, what others think of them. The "bruiser," as Wuest translates, is a self-centered person who seeks to fight or argue his way over those who are threatening. This person's need for validation is more important than his commitment to serve the people. He is not a listener. He is not proactive; he is reactive. Life is about him. In every situation he feels the need to validate his ego-centered position.

This self-centeredness is seen in the leader who demands submission and loyalty. He cannot be challenged and certainly never be corrected. He is surrounded by those who possess weak character and low confidence. He is a master at manipulating the codependent. He always has a scriptural justification for his position and actions. While he may not be a physical striker, he attacks his opponents through the religious political channels. He is feared more than he is loved; he controls more than he leads.

NOT GREEDY OF FILTHY LUCRE

This phrase goes beyond the love of money, which is addressed by another term. This is the person who is eager for gain. The moderate person does not allow any of his desires to become excessive. Pride pushes one to experience an unrealistic need to grow and make gains. I believe the desire to succeed and grow is a part of our God-given nature. I believe the absence of any desire to grow or experience gain is an unhealthy sign. That is counter-balanced by the fact that an obsessive desire to make gains is equally unhealthy.

Proverbs 20:21 says, "*An inheritance may be gotten hastily at the beginning; but the end thereof shall not be blessed.*" The egocentric need for growth has all the appearances of success, but in the end it becomes trouble and pain. The shortcuts to success become the demons that undermine the stability of our position. I recall a particular minister who would go in nearly any direction, start nearly any program if it would give numerical growth to his church. He absorbed several ministries into his organization and experienced rapid growth and even became the standard for success in his city. Yet, his ministry was plagued with turmoil and strife. There were constant power struggles. He confided in me how much he despised the ministry and the people to whom he was called to minister.

Questions I often ask myself about programs and ministerial efforts are, "Do I believe that what I am doing is benefiting people?" and "Will I continue to do this regardless of the lack of personal benefit it brings to me or my church?" These questions serve to keep my motivation within healthy bounds. "What if this benefits another ministry more than it benefits mine?"

Too often, leaders will only support those programs and activities that directly promote growth for their organization. I have seen people cultivate entirely new theological concepts simply because they realized the benefit it would bring. This is a greed-motivated activity, which stands opposed to love-motivated activity. In time, the pain to leaders and followers becomes too great of a price for this short-lived shell of success.

PATIENT

This word is translated as moderate and gentle. A patient person has a sense of responsibility and awareness of the consequences of his actions and decisions. This person stands in contradiction to the brawler, the striker, or the one who lacks honor and moderation. The previous self-serving traits construct a picture of the one who acts hastily, motivated by his ego-driven actions. The patient man, however, is not quick to make decisions. He is free from the impulsiveness that comes from sitting in judgement. Like the wise man in Proverbs, he realizes that the first person always appears to be right. He is not hasty in word, deed or decision.

The patient man is gentle in his behavior and methods. He recognizes that force is an unacceptable method for accomplishing his agenda. The gentle leader attempts to relate to others in a way that does not infringe on their freedom of choice or their sense of self-worth. This does not mean that he is passive or indecisive. He simply knows the difference between his issues and the issues of others.

Some sources present patience as "the ability to

stand under pressure without wavering." The patient leader is a person of conviction not convenience. His beliefs are the basis for the moral fabric of his life. They were forged out of the furnace of life. He is not double-minded. He knows that standing on the truth, motivated by love is the only abiding solution. Short-term gimmicks, trendy fads and crisis management have no appeal to the patient leader. He calmly abides and endures the test of time.

NOT A BRAWLER

This term refers to not being quarrelsome or contentious. The book of Proverbs lists pride, strife, meddling, scorn, anger, foolishness and gossip as the motivating factors behind a quarrelsome attitude.[12] Fools love to quarrel. They love to air their opinions. They need to appear "right." Much of the teaching about showing honor and submission has been nothing more than a vain attempt to create a spiritual justification for the need to appear "right." A congregation who loves their pastor can do so whether they perceive him as right or wrong. This is the fruit of a pastor who loves his people even when they are wrong.

Some translate "patient" as "gentle." The gentle leader does not delight in arguing or winning the argument. He delights, instead, in helping and serving others. We need leaders who are peacemakers. We need those who are willing to lose the argument to save the person. Sometimes the arguer appears to be one who is "apt to teach." In reality, the arguer is not apt to teach within scriptural bounds and motives. He is apt to prove his point. This is the person who will create a "party spirit." The brawler, compelled by the need to be "right," i.e., winning the argument, draws others into a group who takes sides. This person will always produce division and strife.

One of the traits I attempt to develop in leaders is freedom from the need to be "right." This is only done effectively by modeling and patience. I know of few other traits that destroy as many as "the need to be right." Humility is so foreign to the twentieth century church that people will not recognize or believe it unless they see it modeled on a regular basis. It is essential that people see it

---

[12] Proverbs 13:10, 17:14, 18:6, 21:19, 22:10, 26:21

is acceptable to be wrong. The majority of conflict in every situation revolves around someone's need to be "right." Being "right" is not what qualifies us for ministry. It does not bring the blessings of God and it does not give us peace.

NOT COVETOUS

This term literally means, "not a lover of money." Paul told Timothy, *"The love of money is the root of all evil."* Those who love money become mercenaries. They are among those who sell their services to the highest bidder. Once again, this weakness is rarely presented in the most obvious ways, yet the leader with this weakness finds himself/herself being drawn to those who have money. In the statement of ethics for Impact International Fellowship of Ministers, each minister agrees that he will not become involved with those of financial means in a way that will affect the way he makes decisions.

The Bible cautions against giving special privilege or high regard to the wealthy.

"My brethren, have not the faith of our Lord Jesus Christ, the Lord of glory, with respect of persons. For if there come unto your assembly a man with a gold ring, in goodly apparel, and there come in also a poor man in vile raiment; And ye have respect to him that weareth the gay clothing, and say unto him, Sit thou here in a good place; and say to the poor, Stand thou there, or sit here under my footstool: Are ye not then partial in yourselves, and are become judges of evil thoughts? Hearken, my beloved brethren, Hath not God chosen the poor of this world rich in faith, and heirs of the kingdom which he hath promised to them that love him? But ye have despised the poor. Do not rich men oppress you, and draw you before the judgment seats?" James 2:1-6.

Honoring those with resources has become the norm for our day. We mount plaques in their honor. They sit on the platform. They become the personal friends of the minister. Our standard procedures discourage the person of average income while feeding the personal problems of the wealthy. The wealthy need a place where they can have relationships that are not based on their money.

When a wealthy man gives two percent of his income and a poor man gives twenty percent of his, we honor the wealthy as if they had made some great sacrifice.

This is the work of the mercenary who sells his friendship and loyalty to the highest bidder. Jesus addressed this issue in Mark 12:42-44, in the story of the widow's mite. *"And there came a certain poor widow, and she threw in two mites, which make a farthing. And he called unto him his disciples, and saith unto them, Verily I say unto you, That this poor widow hath cast more in, than all they which have cast into the treasury: For all they did cast in of their abundance; but she of her want did cast in all that she had, even all her living."*

This is not to say we should despise the wealthy. However, we should not honor them simply because they have wealth. If an individual has become wealthy by observing Biblical principles, we should open our heart to him because of his wisdom, not his money. When built upon Biblical principles, success should be honored, observed and duplicated. We should help the wealthy to establish a Biblical view of money. They should become faithful stewards over that which has been entrusted to them.

Another aspect of the one whom is a lover of money is that he/she is stingy. He is not a generous, free giver. Everything is about his needs and desires instead of the needs and desires of the people. We want to develop generosity in all of our leaders. A leader should model generosity in every area of life. He should model giving just as he models serving.

ONE THAT RULES WELL HIS OWN FAMILY

This statement could stand-alone. Including the entire verse, however, provides clarity. *"One that ruleth well his own house, having his children in subjection with all gravity; (For if a man know not how to rule his own house, how shall he take care of the church of God."* 1 Timothy 3:4-5. This passage provides opportunity for great insight as well as great misunderstanding.

The first thing we see is the principle, "Who a man is at home is who he really is." Too often we hail the one who has a large ministry and a terrible home life. We are quick to make excuses. Somehow we justify the inconsistencies. I have observed that those who neglect their family for the ministry set a standard that requires others to do the same. Often we find entire groups of followers who justify the same neglect of their family. Too often, we find those who are pursuing fulfillment through the ministry that should be found at home. This person's family is condemned and controlled through a self-serving doctrine. This is the basis of much infidelity in the ministry.

Every family is different. It is impossible and unhealthy to stereotype the perfect family. Once again, however, we are not working a checklist. This is not one who rules his family in a particular way, but one who leads his family in a way that has positive, healthy results; who makes his spouse and children feel loved and that their desires are important. He puts forth effort to promote individual self-worth and decision making in his family. I like to see children allowed to be children instead of pawns that determine the way the leader will be revered.

It is important to realize that we cannot lift this scripture out of the Bible and ignore other passages that provide healthy guidelines for relationships. Too many leaders have used this scripture as a basis to control the entire family. This does not give us the privilege of ignoring the supreme commandment of walking in love. This does not give the spiritual leader the excuse to domi-nate, control or neglect his family for the ministry. One who would destroy the family for the ministry would destroy the people for the ministry.

In this we see a portrait of one who lovingly leads his family. He/she has the respect of the family. The family willingly supports him in his endeavors. Likewise, the family-oriented leader supports his/her children in the endeavors of their choice. A leader is one who inspires others to follow and who teaches and models the truth he represents. If we can successfully develop and lead our family, those who know every flaw and secret, surely we can effectively lead the household of God. The opposite is clear. One who cannot lead his family in a healthy, Biblical way will not be able to do so in the household of God.

In the phrase, "ruling his own family," there is also the hint of providing for his own family. The Bible says that one who does not provide for his family *is worse than an infidel and has denied the faith*. The rush to the full-time ministry has caused many spouses and children to despise the ministry and the minister. A hungry family does not love the ministry.

Ruling one's house is not a dictatorial description of the man of the house. As a matter of fact, a man who rules his family by force is unacceptable to lead in the house of God. Nowhere should leadership be more positive and compelling than in our own family. Too often, the leader's ego is at stake in the actions of his family. He does not lead from love. He leads from ego. He forces his wife and children into some stereotyped role with no consideration for their personal goals and dreams. This type of leadership proves him to be a dream stealer. Although the entire family may be under control, he does not rule his family well.

NOT A NOVICE

The word "novice," according to several sources, means "newly planted." An overseer must not be newly planted in the Lord, in the ministry, or in the local church. Every person should be proven. If one truly has a passion to serve, they will serve without recognition, payment, or position. All of those things come in due time as the fruit of our ministry grows. Those who are motivated by these things are obviously motivated by something other than the desire to serve.

In today's rush to the full-time ministry, we have created a system which looks down on an individual who derives income from personal labor. Therefore, there is an unhealthy sense of urgency about being "in the ministry." It is respectable for a young minister to work to support his call. Why should anyone else support their call if they are not willing to do so? Let every person prove his or her call. Not by getting in the full-time ministry, but by taking the time to walk through a healthy process.

It is not enough that a person is saved for a reasonable length of time, one should also walk in their call for a reasonable length of time without the ego-inflating maze of titles and positions. I had a dear friend who had been in the ministry for years. Many of those years he was not even born again. He got saved, left his denomination and was almost immediately put in a leadership position. Although he was a good man and had many years in the ministry, he was a novice. It was reflected in his teaching and ministerial ineffectiveness.

Likewise, it is important that one who comes to a local body be there for a time before being given a position in the local church. My greatest failures in raising up leaders has come when I hired or brought in those who had served for years in other congregations, yet had not been developed in our system. When I have not required that they be a part of coming up through the process, I have usually regretted it.

The danger for a novice is that he be lifted up with pride. Pride can never be a servant. Pride twists every issue to be "about me." In the original, it literally says, "lest he be wrapped in a mist or a smoke." While there is an obvious illusion to pride, there are a few other considerations about the literal meaning of this phrase.

One being "wrapped in a smoke" is one who cannot be seen as he really is. Over the short term, one can mask many corrupt motives in the mirage of good works. His accomplishments hide his true agendas. Over time, however, the truth cannot be hidden. All things come to light with time. The concept of being wrapped in smoke immediately brings to mind the saying, "Blowing smoke." It is easy for the novice to blow smoke, but not really know. Often we have had Bible school students who thought they were ready to take on the world. They could talk the talk. So they assumed they could walk the walk. They did not know the saying, "The map is not the territory." I remember two such men who launched out to start a church. They were sure of themselves, but it was all smoke. In just a few weeks they gave up. They were not bad, nor were they attempting to deceive. They just could not see for the smoke.

The devil fell into a snare by "reasoning concerning his brightness."[13] In other words, Satan looked at the fact that he had splendor and began to justify his actions. Those judgements took him through a process of reasoning that brought about his fall and the fall of millions. We must all face the fact that our successes do not make us special. They do not justify our weaknesses, nor do they give us any special privileges. The novice has this tendency to fall into this same snare. Unfortunately, no one ever falls alone!

GOOD REPORT OF THEM THAT ARE WITHOUT

Jesus was the friend of sinners. He had a good report among the lost. We must never forget our responsibility to the lost. We can never manage our life and

---

[13] "Satan Unmasked," James B. Richards, Impact International Publications, Huntsville, Alabama

ministry in such a way that brings reproach to the gospel. Too many times the church disregards the lost world through spiritual justification.

In order to have a good report with them that are without, we must be in touch with them. It is essential that a leader never lose touch with the needs of lost humanity. We must remain relevant.[14] When we lose relevance in the world, we have usually lost relevance in the lives of our congregation.

There is, of course, the obvious in this passage. We must manage our business affairs with diligence, honesty and professionalism. When I worked in a music store, the entire staff hated to do business with churches. We all knew that a church group would take more time, buy the cheapest equipment, want the most service and the biggest discount. The world does not owe us a discount because we are Christians. We should consider our scope of influence as important as the money we save. The Bible teaches that a good name is more valuable than treasure.

A LOVER OF GOOD MEN

This qualification comes from the book of Titus. A leader cannot be one who embraces or promotes the immoral, the unethical, or the controller. *"Blessed is the man that walketh not in the counsel of the ungodly..."* Psalm 1:1 A very large ministry wanted me to help them publish a book. I arranged a meeting between a writer and their ministry leaders. In that meeting we found that many of those who made the decisions for the ministry were not saved nor were they even godly. We quickly walked away from that project. In a few short years the leader of that ministry fell in national disgrace. A contributing factor to his downfall was the fact that he embraced and was advised by men of low character. He assumed their business skills alone qualified them.

In the present political environment it seems that it is permissible to allow staff members to do the dirty work. That way, we cannot be accused. Our hands are clean! It is not enough, however, that we keep our motives and actions free from destructive leadership tendencies. We must never allow these tendencies to continue in our staff

---

[14] *"Relevant Ministry Workbook"*, James B. Richards, Impact International Publications, Huntsville, Alabama

simply because they facilitate our needs. We must develop those around us in a way that produces the kind of leaders who can be trusted with the life and emotions of the people.

The Old Testament presents the concept of "responsibility to rescue." When it is within our power to rescue and we do not, we are as guilty as the one who commits the crime. This principle of responsibility to rescue should be carried into our leadership philosophy. We should intervene when the people are being controlled or taken advantage of by other leaders.

Likewise, those with whom we desire to be, is a reflection of what we desire to be. Our fellowship should be with good, mature, responsible people. We should surround ourselves with those who challenge us to moral, ethical, and responsible behavior. There is nothing that will influence our morals more than those with whom we fellowship. My every decision is in part the product of the character of my leadership team. *"Do not be misled: Bad company corrupts good character."* 1 Corinthians 15:33. NIV.

This character sketch should represent the qualities we desire to develop in all people. The process for becoming a disciple is the same process as becoming a leader. Those who rise to leadership are those who model these characteristics; therefore, they will lead others in this same path. I have found that those who have no commitment to these traits tend to "play them down." Their heart will not allow them to lead others where they do not intend to go. Thus to minimize these standards will minimize our effectiveness in future generations of disciples and leaders.

Questions for the heart:

As we read these traits, there are questions we should ask at each point.

1. Are these the traits I desire to see in the leaders who serve with me? Make a list of present leaders and indicate each trait where they seem to be lacking.

2. How can I develop these traits in my present leadership team?

3. Meet with current leaders and discuss these traits with them. Allow each person to discuss where they feel the desire to develop.

4. Have I elevated my own list of traits above this list?

5. Is my concept of the effective leader really Biblically based?

6. Do I understand the role each of these traits plays in developing effectiveness in ministry? Think about how each of these traits will strengthen a person's ministry.

7. Do I value these traits in my personal life?

8. Do I model these traits to my leaders?

SECTION 4

THE PROCESS OF PROMOTION

For too long the church has failed to work the clearly established agenda given by the Lord Himself. We are to make disciples. Winning the lost is not the goal. It is a part of the continuum of discipleship. Getting miracles is not the goal. Deliverance is not the goal. Building churches is not the goal. Developing leaders is not the goal. All of these are essential aspects of the continuum.[1]

Taking a clearly prescribed Biblical directive and making it the goal of ministry is so deceitful. Because it is in the Bible its cause can be argued. But the cause must be differentiated from the process. The highest personal call of an individual is to have a relationship with God. The highest functional call is to become a disciple. We must never allow serving to supercede relationship, yet we should never accept the concept of a healthy relationship apart from discipleship, which takes one into the arena of personal service.

As early as possible one must attempt to place an individual in an area of service. The area of service should match their personal growth, character, interest and ability. However, a person will never really grow if they are only learning information. The greatest growth comes when teaching is coupled with opportunity to serve. This is where people truly develop. This is where they come to feel like a real part of the church family. Those who never serve, seldom ever feel secure in their relationship with the church family. They become more like a spoiled child who never works with the other family members and never feels like they belong

Always match their skills and interests with an area of ministry. The area of ministry may be working on cars for widows. It may be walking through the parking lot during a church service for safety patrol. It may be a part of yard work or a cleaning detail. It may be working on computers. But as soon as possible we want that new believer to be in a reciprocal relationship with the church.

---

[1] The individual's highest responsibility is a personal relationship with God. The church cannot build that. The church is to make disciples. A relationship with God is the essential prerequisite for this process to work.

The concept of serving must be presented early so it will be a part of their Christian belief system. However, it must be a developed concept. The new believer should never feel they are earning approval or spirituality. We must avoid a codependent system where dysfunctional people can rise to power. We must teach and model healthy perspectives of serving.

The best way to develop a person is to never teach him or her beyond what you have given them the opportunity to experience. If people immediately apply what they learn it will have more value and reality. In other words, do not take them through a six-month teaching session about serving while they sit and listen. Give them the opportunity to serve while their faith and excitement is still fresh and new.

Teach a little; work a little. When there is implementation, there is no room for deceit. You know who is serious and who is not. This separates the talkers from the doers. There are a lot of talkers out there. They have great potential. Their story and potential coupled with our eagerness to get people active causes us to depend on them prematurely. This is a major source of leadership frustration for the leader and the feeling of pressure for the follower.

Be good at matching people with tasks. Make sure the task is not beneath or above the person. Either situation will be de-motivating. Make sure the task is equal to their spiritual maturity. We have falsely assumed that those who were faithful in natural things should be promoted to handle spiritual things. That is only partially true.

We have another false concept that a good worker will make a good leader. The Bible warns against a servant ruling. Leading is a gift and a skill. When a good servant tries to lead he will frustrate those who are attempting to follow and he will frustrate himself. When he cannot handle the task he may become indignant and leave.

Make sure a person is adequately trained for the task. The level of training will determine the level of success. Failure to train conveys a lack of importance for the task and the person. Take the time to slowly develop people. We may need them in places of service today, but we want more than warm bodies. We want them to know how to do the task at hand. But more importantly we want the place of service to stimulate growth not discourage it.

NOTES

Turn over is very bad for any business or ministry. A constant turnover in workers and leaders sends a message of instability. People will begin to doubt your programs and your leadership. They will be afraid to get their hopes up. They will hold back from participation. They want to see if new programs are going to make it or not. The wait and see attitude causes the death of many worthy projects. It is better to have a lack in some area of your ministry than to prematurely begin a ministry that will fail. Take the time to develop your ministry by taking the time to develop your leaders.

After selecting the right people for the right task, there is the process of training, promotion and ongoing support. All of these are essential aspects of developing and maintaining healthy, productive leaders. This section takes you through this process in an understandable way.

11

MODELING

As I read the New Testament, I am amazed that the church has survived the first decade. Jesus spent a little more than three years with a group of twelve men, all of whom had personal problems. They fought among themselves. They struggled for power and position. Jesus, Himself, rebuked them for unbelief and hardness of heart. Yet, 2000 years later the church is here. The seed that Jesus planted was not lost through inept leaders. Despite their personal problems that continued until their death, they fulfilled their call.

In the book of Acts we are told that Paul went into an area, got people saved, taught and developed them, ordained leaders and left. These novices successfully assumed great responsibilities. This is unheard of in our generation. If we left a new church in the hands of new converts it would be disastrous. Yet, out of these seemingly impossible scenarios, powerful churches arose that endured and influenced the world for centuries.

If we are not getting the same results, we must concede to the possibility that we are leaving something out of our equation in developing leaders. There must be some vital link that we are missing. There is-modeling! Jesus and Paul relied heavily on modeling to develop potential leaders. Modeling is an impossibility in the typical church mentality that insists that leaders should not be too close to the people.

Our distance from the leader is what sustains the false elevation of the minister above the people. This is a continuation of the clergy-laity hierarchy. This system was not devised to develop or benefit the people. The mystical elevation of the minister provides a basis for control. Once the leader is placed on the pedestal he is afraid to allow the people to see his frailties. In the end, however, this always backfires. The elevation of the "clergy" makes ministry seem unattainable. Once people put you on a pedestal they want you to live up to their expectations. And finally, you can never develop people by modeling. In their minds you are too far above them. They could never attain the effectiveness of the man of God.

Paul's success in raising up leaders started with selecting qualified people. He chose those who fit into the character sketch that he gave Timothy. Like Jesus, he taught them the Word. But over a prolonged period of time, he modeled how they should live and function. They saw how he handled the people, the successes, the pressures and the failures. In 2 Timothy 3:10-11, Paul told Timothy, *"But thou hast fully known my doctrine, manner of life, purpose, faith, longsuffering, charity, patience, persecutions, afflictions, which came unto me at Antioch, at Iconium, at Lystra; what persecutions I endured: but out of them all the Lord delivered me."*

Timothy had seen it all. He had traveled with Paul. In those areas where Paul did not have a person to leave in charge, he would often stay for as long as two years. Healthy modeling was a key ingredient of the success of the early church. Often, he would leave someone who had been developed through the modeling process. This element is absent from the present day mentality. We take the potential leader into a classroom, teach him a few lessons and never have personal involvement. Yet, we expect him to know how to handle the complexities of ministering to people with very complex needs.

Be assured that we started developing our potential leaders long before we ever brought them into our team. Our developmental process began by what they saw us do the first day they came to our church. Potential leaders watch the current leaders. From their behavior, they develop a paradigm through which they will interpret everything that is taught.

It is essential to remember that when verbal and non-verbal communications disagree, the non-verbal is what people believe to be true. How we handle people, how we act under pressure, what we do when we are angry, all communicate volumes of information to those who observe. This is the real truth! This is what we really believe! From observation more than teaching, others determine what they consider our true beliefs.

Another place people identify our true values is through the stories we tell. The stories we tell reflect what we actually value. Story telling is the glorification of past events. When we tell a story about proving someone wrong, winning an argument, or about being right, we are conveying our value for being right. We are expressing our exploits of conquering and controlling others. If that is what we value, it will be what our followers will value.

When we bring on a new team member, we have already determined how they interpret our didactic teaching. We teach them about serving and walking in love. All the while their mind is saying, "Yeah, I know what you really mean. You really mean what I have seen you do. You mean it is all right to do what we want as long as we say the right things."

Western culture is the only culture that has no value for the apprenticeship program. The consequences are seen in the youth of today. Mentoring is a lost concept. We are information mongers. We attempt to solve every problem with more information. We fail to understand the dynamics of the human process. Fathers do not model to their children, few companies still have apprenticeship programs. We have higher education, which produces young people with a head full of knowledge and no wisdom. The man with the degree gets ahead even if he has no life experience. Even when his abilities do not equal his degree, he is the one who gets the promotion. We encourage the development of fools.

Paul modeled the principles of leadership to Timothy and he encouraged Timothy to continue in that same method of teaching. Timothy faced difficulties in his ministry. Paul never told him to use authority as the way to solve a problem; nor did he tell him to rely on teaching alone. Instead Paul told Timothy to teach and model the truth. *"Similarly, encourage the young men to be self-controlled. In everything **set them an example** by doing what is good. In your teaching show integrity, seriousness and soundness of speech that cannot be condemned, so that those who oppose you may be ashamed because they have nothing bad to say about us."* Titus 2:6-8, NIV. *"Don't let anyone look down on you because you are young, but set an example for the believers in speech, in life, in love, in faith and in purity."* 1 Timothy 4:12, NIV.

In our attempt to present truth, we are always working through the other person's paradigms. They are interpreting everything we say in light of those personal, predetermined concepts. This means there is often a huge gap between what we are saying and what they think we are saying. Even when the concepts are properly understood there is still a problem in understanding the application. All of these problems are effectively eradicated through modeling. Teach a man what to do, and he may

98

forget. Show a man what to do, then let him do it and he will get it right.

Paul saw the life of Christ as a place to see the Christian life modeled. The mercy of God was taught in the Old Testament, but the people never comprehended it. When Isaiah said, "*My thoughts are not your thoughts and my ways are not your ways*," he was specifically referring to God's complete mercy for the sinner. The Jews never saw the mercy. Jesus came as a man and modeled the realities of God's character. Paul said that God's mercy on him should serve as a model for the entire church world. "*Here is a trustworthy saying that deserves full acceptance: Christ Jesus came into the world to save sinners—of whom I am the worst. But for that very reason I was shown mercy so that in me, the worst of sinners, Christ Jesus might display his unlimited patience as an example for those who would believe on him and receive eternal life.*" 1 Timothy 1:15-16, NIV.

Too often we read the epistles and extrapolate doctrines that not only deny the finished work of the cross, but deny the very life that Jesus modeled. When we read the Gospel we must look at the examples as much as the doctrine. It is easy to misunderstand the doctrine, but impossible to misunderstand the behavior that Jesus modeled. Too often we lift the words out of the real life context and lose their meaning.

There should be nothing taught in our leadership development process that is not modeled. This sometimes makes the difference between leaders and managers. We should not manage people, but lead them. We manage time and resources, but we never manage people. Management is about taking control. We should take control of ourselves, our time, and our resources. We should plan and use our time and resources to fulfill our personal agendas. But we should never use people; we should lead people. Modeling is the first step in leading people. It establishes a never-ending cycle that initiates and develops a bond between teachers and students.

Leadership is simply walking ahead of people. As leaders, we create the path for others to follow. We demonstrate how it is done. We make followers feel safe and secure in the pathway. We do not point people in a direction; we lead in a direction. Moses did not stand at the Red Sea and say, "Go that way." He led them across on dry land. Just as those people needed to feel safe about

NOTES

walking in the midst of the sea, we must make our co-leaders feel safe about where they are asked to walk. We need to show them the safety in being servants. This concept is so foreign to the natural mind that it is inconceivable. We must model every step of this process.

In our local church program, a new convert gets a sponsor who models Christianity to them. The disciple gets an Impact Leader who models to them. The worker has a leader who models to them. The leader has a staff member who models to them. The staff members have me as the senior pastor modeling to them. There should never be a part of the process where a person does not have a role model.

Paul modeled financial responsibility to the Thessalonians. *"For you yourselves know how you ought to follow our **example**. We were not idle when we were with you, nor did we eat anyone's food without paying for it. On the contrary, we worked night and day, laboring and toiling so that we would not be a burden to any of you. We did this, not because we do not have the right to such help, but in order to make ourselves a model for you to follow. For even when we were with you, we gave you this rule: If a man will not work, he shall not eat."* 2 Thessalonians 3:7-10, NIV.

Paul pointed out that they were models to the lost world. *"And so you became a model to all the believers in Macedonia and Achaia."* 1 Thessalonians 1:7, NIV. Like us, they did not realize that they were modeling for anyone. Whether we want to or not, we are marking the path for someone. Parents model to their children. Church members model to their fellow employees. It never ends! Jesus said, *"You are the light of the world."* (Whether you want to be or not.) You will either be a bright light that makes the path clear and safe, or a dim light that makes the path dangerous and destructive.[1]

The current attitude of the world toward the church has been the product of preaching one message and modeling another. The world does not believe our words because our life proclaims something else much louder. I believe we could live more and preach less and be much more effective. The world does not need to hear about God's love; they need to see and experience it through the

---

[1] *"Supernatural Ministry, Unleashing the Gifts Within You,"* James B. Richards, Impact International Publications, Huntsville, Alabama

church.

Paul was not an egomaniac. He was simply a committed Christian. He did not do everything right. To the Philippians he said "*Join with others in following my example, brothers, and take note of those who live according to the pattern we gave you.*" Philippians 3:17, NIV. To the Corinthian believers he said, "*Follow my example, as I follow the example of Christ.*" 1 Corinthians 10:33, NIV. Paul learned this secret, "the life of the minister is the life of the ministry." He did not live his life one away and his ministry another. The ministry was a continuum of his life. Therefore, all of the programs he developed were congruent with his life. Everything in his life and ministry said, "Follow me!"

Questions for the heart:

1. Is modeling a planed part of my discipleship and leadership development?

2. Who do I allow to get close enough to me to be a role model for them?

3. What are my fears about allowing people to get too close?

4. How do people react when they see him up close?

5. What does this say about my relationship with people?

6. Do the people in my church keep me on a pedestal?

7. What have I done to have a more realistic relationship with the people?

8. What value could come in people knowing the real me?

9. Am I different around church people and around my friends?

10. How?

11. How do I plan to start the modeling process in my ministry/organization?

12

THE COMMISSION OF A LEADER

Someone has said, "A good start, guarantees a good finish." How we start determines how it goes. The seeds of success or destruction are planted in the way you begin. To insure a good start, every person must have a clear commission and quality training consistent with the commission. The quality of training provided in the beginning speaks volumes about the importance of the task.

If I am trained, I understand there are rules, goals, principles and boundaries. I am able to find the help and support I need. The quality of training defines my perception of the job quality you expect. Proper training insures the boundaries will exist to provide a sense of security, direction and accomplishment. Among the things that must be established in the earliest phases of job training is the mission statement. I must know what I am attempting to accomplish. What is the commission? What exactly, do you want me to accomplish? How do you want it accomplished? What techniques can I use? How much creative freedom do I have? How will I be evaluated? How will you measure my success? How will I be rewarded? These are all things every team member must know.[1]

In addition to all of the above, I want the team member to know and accept the Biblical commission given to leaders[2] in the scripture. *"And he gave some, apostles; and some, prophets; and some, evangelists; and some, pastors and teachers; For the perfecting of the saints, for the work of the ministry, for the edifying of the body of Christ."* Ephesians 4:11-12. This is God's job description, His commission for leaders. It is the only leadership plan God has. It is the leader's commission. Just as those who join themselves with me must be sure their personal vision is compatible and consistent with mine, I must be sure we

---

[1] In an earlier chapter we discussed the fact that they must also know how they will fulfill their dreams within your organization. This is the ultimate prerequisite for becoming a team member.

[2] Everyone on the team is a leader at some level. The children's pastor leads the workers. The worker leads the children. So it is in every area of the ministry.

NOTES

are all compatible and consistent with God's commission.

I want every leader to plan for and expect numerical growth. Proverbs says, "*In the multitude of people is the king's honour: but in the want of people is the destruction of the prince.*" Proverbs 14:28. Every leader desires and expects numerical growth. But that growth does not supercede the commission to equip, mend and make whole the people of God. If my vision is to build a large church, I could begin to use people to fulfill my vision. I could make them give up their vision and accept mine. I could give little attention to their personal growth and development. I could use all of their personal skills and resources and then discard them when they have nothing left to give. All of this would be justified in the name of the vision. All the while I assume I am fulfilling the plan of God. In actuality, I am only fulfilling my own plan.

There would be nothing wrong with the vision to build a large church if the motivating purpose behind that vision was to perfect, mend, and make whole the saints, and then launch them into serving. The process would qualify the vision. And the purpose would provide the message instead of the vision providing the message. I have been in many churches where the message was really about the church growing numerically. Instead, however, the church should grow because of a message that benefits the people in their walk with God and their journey through life.

Because our message seems to spring from our personal vision more than our call, there are some strange messages proclaimed and embraced. The church is very confused about the plan of God for their life. Every minister is trying to pull every person into their personal plan for serving God instead of serving the people so they can fulfill their call and passion. Paul faced this very dilemma. "*For I have no man likeminded, who will naturally care for your state. For all seek their own, not the things which are Jesus Christ's.*" Philippians 2:20-21. Selfish ambition and personal vision have plagued the church since the earliest times.

In many instances when the Bible talks about vision, it is talking about a clear mental picture. We tend to assume that our vision is from the Lord. The call, as described in Ephesians 4:11-12, is from the Lord. This is God's vision. Our personal vision is the result of our own desires, preferences, gifts and skills. If your gifting is in the area of personal counsel, that gifting will give birth to a clear mental picture about counseling. You may desire to develop a counseling center. That is fine as long as the motive and goal for having that center is to make people whole so they can find their place of ministry.

It is the same with any area of gifting. That gifting causes us to have a passion in a certain area. That passion and insight produces our vision. But too often, we confuse our vision with God's call. If we are a part of the five-fold ministry, God has clearly described our call/commission. We will simply fulfill that call in the area that we have a gift, passion or desire. Regardless of the office or gifting we are servants. Our office or gifts simply clarify how and where we will serve. It does not change the goal of our service.

The moment our gifting becomes the motivation behind our ministry we will stop using the ministry to develop people and begin using people to develop our ministry. Regardless of which gift or office we use to get there, Ephesians 4:11-12 must be our destination. Any other destination is going to be a self-serving, selfish ambition. In James 3:16 it says, *"For where envying and strife is, there is confusion and every evil work."* The word translated "envy" could actually be translated as "zeal." Zeal is not usually a positive thing in the scripture. It speaks of a person being driven from selfish ambition. Where there is selfish ambition there is confusion and every evil work. If the call of the minister is not to give and serve, it will ultimately be to take and use.

We may have a passion to reach 10,000 souls per month. Regardless of the good that comes from accomplishing that goal, within the ministry and within the heart of the minister one may encounter some very unattractive motives. That goal, if forced to stand alone, is not consistent with the commission God gives to leaders. On the other hand, the goal to reach 10,000 souls per month that is motivated by and governed by the desire to make people whole and see them find their place of service will glorify God and benefit the people. It will be structured around goals and procedures that will produce positive results in the lives of the people.

Over the years I have seen teaching ministries that had the transferring of information as their goal. After all, isn't that what teachers do; Teach? Yes it is, but that can all become an egocentric end within itself. The emphasis can be placed on our revelation, what we know, or what new revelations we have. The end of that kind of motivation is always error and confusion. It is motivated by the need to impress instead of helping people become whole and launched into meaningful service. The church's commission is to reach the world and make disciples of them. The leader's commission is to accomplish that goal by perfecting, i.e., making others whole and launching them into the area of service they desire. When one departs from this God-given agenda, he may preach truth, but he can still lead people away from God's plan for fulfillment.[3]

This is the reason the New Testament equates false teachers of the New Testament with the false prophets of the Old Testament. It was the false prophet more than the teacher that led people astray in the Old Testament. The Law was pretty "cut and dried." There was not much to explain about the information. So, the false prophet led people astray about what they claimed to have heard from God. In the New Testament we are dealing with truth that must be understood and applied from the heart. This makes it quite easy to get mystical with truth. It becomes easy to mask it in all sorts of unscriptural agendas that lead the people from God's ultimate goal. It is easy for the leader to present wonderful truth that leads people away from God's clearly established plan.

One of the greatest products of the charismatic movement was the restoration of the teaching ministry. One of the worst products of the charismatic move was the restoration of the teaching ministry. While many people responded to teaching in a positive, healthy way, others ushered us into the era that the Bible described as a dark time for mankind. "*For the time will come when they will not endure sound doctrine; but after their own lusts shall they heap to themselves teachers, having itching ears;*" 2 Timothy 4:3. Paul describes a type of person who is, "*Ever learning, and never able to come to the knowledge of the truth.*" 2 Timothy 3:7. This is the product of a teacher who always has a new revelation and a listener who never gets involved in implementation.

The transference of information that is not pointed

---

[3] Keep in mind that wholeness and discipleship revolve around a personal relationship with the Lord. I am not implying that serving God supercedes knowing God. Actually the two grow hand in hand. One without the other eventually becomes vain religion.

toward causing people to be mended, made whole and ultimately serving God's people is crippling. It nourishes self-centeredness. It promotes codependency. It elevates the minister and his knowledge to the source of truth instead of the Holy Spirit. The believer then looks to the minister as the source instead of God and begins the endless search to discover the ultimate truth. Because, after all, more information is what he thinks he needs for victory. The twentieth-century Christian seems to be walking about looking for that ultimate truth that will make everything all right. This attitude is a breeding ground for error and destruction.

Every office of the five-fold ministry can become extremely warped and self-serving if one does not distinguish the difference between God's clearly described commission and our personal vision. We must judge and mold our every effort in the ministry to comply with the parameters of Ephesians 4:11-12. We must reach people and do what it takes to mend (perfect) them so they can do the work of the ministry. Leave out one element of the commission and trouble will abound.

After having been "proved" as a servant and growing in the character traits of an effective leader, a new team member should be trained and provided a clear, understandable commission of the task they are undertaking. Take nothing for granted. Utilize two-way communication to make sure they understand the job and its demands. Make verbal and written agreements about the goals and commitments being made. Written agreements do not make anything more binding, nor is that the purpose. Written agreements make things clear. I have actually had failing leaders say, "I knew we agreed to do it this way, but I did not think you meant it." When things are put in writing, people believe you mean it!

Discuss how their personal passions will fit into the commission of Ephesians 4:11-12. Let them explain how they will fulfill their goals within the framework of your calling and goals. Make sure you know their short term and long term goals. Make sure you have a commitment about how long they will be with you. Start with a clear commission and commitment. How you start determines how you finish!

Questions for the heart:

1. Did I provide a clear commission for all current workers and leaders? If not, meet with each one and discuss the commission.

2. Emphasize how this plan will fulfill God's commission.

3. Allow the person to talk about their vision and how it fits into this plan.

4. Explain the difference between your personal vision and God's vision.

5. Develop mission's statements for every area of the ministry.

6. Does every team member receive adequate training before they begin working in their area?

7. Do I allow them to evaluate that training?

8. What type of training programs do I need to start?

9. Do I provide ongoing training? How am I presently doing that?

10. How am I making sure the worker is still receiving personal ministry?

13

NURTURING

Nurturing is probably one of the most overlooked and challenging areas of developing and maintaining leaders. This was certainly an area that I did not understand or develop until recently. Yet, it has become the richest area of ministry for my staff and me. According to Funk and Wagnall, nurture is that which nourishes. To nurture is to feed, strengthen, train, build up, etc. Just as Jesus nurtured the twelve, all leaders must nurture those they serve. This is especially true of the senior leader and his leadership team. We must make a life-long commitment to nourish those around us.

Just as the body consumes the fuel of nourishment through daily activity, likewise, those who serve consume emotional and spiritual energy. Those who work with troubled people sometimes get their focus on the trouble instead of the solution. The emotional drain of working with people is phenomenal. Burnout is at an all time high. There are thousands of reasons why people need nurturing.

We do not nurture people because they have become weak and frail. We nurture them because they are active, because they are giving and because we want them to continue to grow. Many leaders abandon their personal development and place all of their attention on helping others. Too often, they deplete themselves and do not get needed support from their leader. In our current impersonal world it seems that the senior leaders want to pass on intellectual instruction in a seminar and then retreat to the golf course. Too often we think that having given the information is enough.

Like many, I spent much of my life thinking that nurturing was just for the weak. I wanted strong people around me. I wanted those who could carry their load with little input from me. My warped paradigm prevented me from the very thing I desired, strong leaders. I failed to see that planting a leader is like planting a tree. If it is to become and stay strong it must have nourishment. While it is true that a leader should know how to encourage himself, I still have a moral and ethical responsibility to minister to him/her.

As a "high achiever" I felt internal, self-imposed

pressure to accomplish certain tasks. This unhealthy sense of responsibility made me feel that I was wasting my time, if I spent too much time with staff members and not enough time accomplishing tasks. I failed to realize one of the greatest laws of leadership, multiplication. Through the principle of multiplication I accept the reality that I can accomplish much more through people than I can alone. To accomplish through and with people you must be willing to have a slow start. It is always slower to invest in others at the beginning. It takes time to teach them what you know and organize them to productive action. You could be out doing it all yourself, today!

Through the law of multiplication I accept the fact that a slow start that involves and develops others is a sure start. In the end, I have more time for personal accomplishments if I invest more quality time into those around me. If everyone around me is living their dream, I will certainly be a success. This requires a deep sense of personal security. If I invest in others, they will have more personal accomplishments. They will do many of the things I desire to do. And worse, they will get the credit. A secure leader invests in others who accomplish more tasks than the leader. Each person in the process accepts their role to accomplish the law of multiplication. To enter the multiplication phase we must surrender ego-driven leadership styles. Leaders invest in and lead others. If we are not investing in others we are not a leader; we are just a high achiever. A high achiever and a leader are not the same thing.

One of my first hurdles was understanding the difference between encouragement and nurturing. I always thought nurturing was for the weak and encouragement was for the strong, but it was just the opposite. Nurturing is for those who will allow themselves to be developed; encouragement is for those who have not yet committed to success. Nurturing is for those who are running the race; encouragement is for those who have not yet decided to run. You only fertilize (nurture) the seed after it is planted.

I found myself encouraging those who were already committed. I am sure they felt I was being superficial. It is sort of like the cheerleaders trying to get the team to score after the game is over and the team has won. On the other hand, I was giving a lot of personal time and attention, attempting to nurture those who had not yet really decided they even wanted to play in the game. In the end,

I would have tremendous investment in them and they did not even show up for the game. As I shared in *"Leadership That Builds People, Volume I,"* I was attempting to do for people what God Himself would not do for them. I was burning myself out on those who had never made a commitment. I felt frustrated and they felt pressured. I am sure they even felt manipulated. I hear this same scenario from preachers around the world.

We must commit our nurturing to those who have committed to God and to the cause. We must not allow those who labor to languish while we give our support to those who are not sure what they want to do. We must follow the simple scriptural principle, *"Invest in good ground!"* Encourage and love those who have not committed, but invest in and nurture those who are laying down their life with you. Too often we neglect the ones we can help and give ourselves to those we cannot help.

I must model the servanthood that I teach. I must serve my leaders. I must be committed to helping them fulfill their goals and dreams. I must continually find ways to invest in them. They must have spiritual and emotional support that is unfailing. Staff meetings are a place where much of this happens. Staff meetings are the private church services for my leaders. This is a safe place where they know they can share and receive. I want my team to walk away from every staff meeting feeling more equipped, encouraged and confident. Staff meetings are not the place to deal with negatives. It is the place to build and strengthen.

Every week I prayerfully search for meaningful things to share with our team of leaders. I am committed to contributing to the quality of their life. This is how we spend the majority of our time. Then a minimal, yet ample, amount of time is spent developing our strategies for ministry to the body. There is regular discussion and open evaluation of our services, my messages, the worship and every area of our ministry. Nothing is untouchable. In an environment of trust there is very little that must be guarded. If there are negatives that must be confronted, that will be done privately after the staff meeting. I never want to injure a person's self-worth, especially before their peers. I never want a team member to have any dread or fear about coming to these meetings.

In addition to the staff meetings, when possible, it can mean so much to sit down one-on-one with each team member. Besides the group investment, I want to make a personal investment. People do not expect you to give them massive amounts of time. They know you have work to do and they have work to do too. But just knowing that your leadership team has first priority in your schedule does so much.

There is an old proverb that says, "A man who waits to go to the doctor until he is sick is like a man who waits to dig the well until he is thirsty." Likewise, it says, "A doctor who waits until the patient is sick to treat them is the lowest kind of doctor." In our society we are plagued with small problems that grow out of proportion. The people do not solve their problems when they are small, but the leaders do not notice them until they are large. In both cases it is a mere lack of sensitivity and foresight that allows problems to grow. A wise leader anticipates the needs of those he serves. Through prayer and meaningful conversation the wise leader becomes aware of needs before they grow out of proportion. And to quote another saying, "An ounce of prevention is worth a pound of cure." Every problem can be easily solved when it is small.

The vigilant leader sees and nurtures his team members before they become too weak to carry the load. He is interested in them because they are people more than the job they do. Through nurturing there is a love and trust that bonds them together beyond any common cause or denominational tie. Nurturing produces the kind of reciprocal trust and commitment that the legalist can never demand. The experienced farmer anticipates the seasonal changes. Based on his foresight he waters, fertilizes, weeds and poisons the predators to insure the healthy development of the crop. Likewise, an experienced leader anticipates the needs of his team and acts accordingly. *"The prudent see danger and take refuge, but the simple keep going and suffer for it."* Proverbs 27:12, NIV. If you want a seed to grow and bear fruit, it is actually quite simple; plant it in good ground, water and fertilize it. It will grow! This is nurturing!

Questions for the heart:

1. Does my need to accomplish tasks keep me from investing in people?

2. Describe your emotions when another staff member succeeds and is honored.

3. Do I find myself investing in those who are not committed?

4. Does the squeaky wheel tend to get the grease?

5. Define nurturing.

6. How am I nurturing my staff?

7. What is the goal of my staff meetings?

   A. Are they positive?

   B. Do they benefit the person as well as the organization?

   C. Does the staff enjoy the staff meetings?

8. How much personal time do I devote to my leaders?

9. Do I become aware of the needs in people's lives before or after they become problems?

10. Do I demand commitment or do I allow it to grow from meaningful relationships?

14

RESOLVING CONFLICT

Resolving conflict is an essential skill for the leader. The leader who does not resolve conflict in an expeditious and equitable manner will never have peace. Therefore, the effective leader must develop healthy, positive concepts about conflict, confrontation and resolution. This is not an area for the fearful or self-centered. It is rare that one can resolve conflict and remain within their comfort zone.

There are two areas of conflict the leader will face. There is external and internal conflict. External conflict is focused outward toward other organizations or individuals. External conflict is often tolerated and even encouraged in some organizations. Having a sectarian attitude creates a false sense of loyalty for the insecure leader. External conflict is not perceived as a threat to the organization or the leader. If allowed to continue it will usually come back to haunt you.

The Bible strictly forbids the "party spirit." There is no room in the Kingdom of God for divisive sectarianism. The short-sighted leader fails to understand that this type of attitude reflects a deep emotional problem that could just as easily turn on a fellow staff member, the senior leader or the organization. Those who are presently loyal to your party and against all others, are attempting to meet a need in their own insecurity. If you fail to live up to their expectations they will turn on you and align with another.

We falsely assume they are on our side because they perceive us as being right. On the contrary, they are on our side because they think that forming a "party-alliance" proves them to be right. If they need to side with someone else to feel right, they will do so and turn on you. Good cannot come from evil. Jesus said, "*...a bad tree cannot bear good fruit.*" Matthew 7:18. A sinful attitude should not be tolerated, even when it is directed outward and seems to fulfill our objectives.

When a staff member enters into external conflict, we should view this as an opportunity to minister to a need. We must also recognize that if that need is not met, it will one day be a problem that we will encounter on some internal level. We do the person and the organization an injustice when we allow sectarian or superiority attitudes to flourish.

The second source of conflict is internal. One form of internal conflict is inter-staff conflict. In this situation staff members have conflict with one another. The leader must be careful to observe the most basic laws of healthy communication if he is to actually resolve conflict and bring about restoration. Proverbs 18:17 NIV says, "*The first to present his case seems right.*" Too often, the first to present their case to the boss is the one who wins. They persuade us to see their point of view. A wise counselor realizes, however, that how you see it is just that, how you see it. That does not mean that is the way it is. He does not assume that either party is lying simply because they both have a different account of what is happening. They both see it from their own perspective.

This passage continues to say, "*...till another comes forward and questions him.*" Once we hear both sides our view could completely change. When someone presents their difficulty to us we should never offer comfort on the basis of believing them to be right. Our comfort should come from the perspective that we will help them resolve their conflict. I once sat down with a "fallen" minister who asked for help. She kept telling me all the unfair things her mate had done. Her previous dealing with ministers convinced her that she had to prove herself to be the victim in order to receive help and mercy.

As our conversation went on, I finally interrupted her and said, "I do not care if it was his fault or your fault. If you want help, I will help." Every time she went back into justifying herself by her husband's failures, I stopped her and said, "I do not need to know that to help you." She became so offended that she left without having one appointment with me. A person's need to prove their side tells me they are more interested in being right than resolving conflict.

Offering comfort to someone on the basis of believing his or her side of the story creates a very unhealthy environment. People need to see that it really does not matter who is right or wrong. The goal is to resolve the conflict and restore people involved. If you need to be right for me to take your side, I may force you to lie. It certainly forces you into the need to be right. Being right never brings peace. When being right is emphasized more

115

than love, peace and relationships, a mean, hard, deceitful attitude is encouraged.

The person who will resolve conflict must be a person of peace. They must have value for peace. They must approach every conflict in a way that promotes peace and resolution. The Bible says, *"Blessed are the peacemakers for they shall see God."* I believe there is a general truth here that says, blessed are the peacemakers for they shall see! See what? Obviously, they shall see God, but I believe they will see God in the situation. They will see the truth. When we are not in peace we cannot see anything but our point of view. We cannot see who we are hurting. We cannot see where we are being deceived. We cannot see why others are angry. We cannot see the solutions. We cannot see any options. Worst of all, we cannot see God or His direction in the situation.

The disciples were sure their boat would sink. They thought God had abandoned them. They were in near hysteria, all the while the Prince of Peace was with them. They could not trust the one who had the power to save because they surrendered their peace to their fear. Peace, on the other hand, sees God and His options. Peace hears the still, small voice.

The peacemaker resolves conflict by encouraging people to walk in love. When people are committed to walking in love, they do the right thing. In Luke, chapter 12, a young man came to Jesus who was in conflict with his family about an inheritance. Like many who come for counsel, he simply wanted Jesus to take his side. He wanted to use Jesus' counsel as leverage against his brother. Jesus never addressed who was right or wrong in the situation.

Jesus' response to the man modeled the only healthy role a counselor can take, *"Who made me a judge or a divider over you?"* When we attempt to decide who is right, we become a judge. The Bible forbids us the right of judgement. Jesus began to address the issue of greed. This was not an assumption that the man was being greedy. Jesus simply gave Him the truth he needed to judge his own motives. Unless the man dealt with the issues of greed in his own heart, he would never reach a peaceful resolution with his brother.

A wise leader takes people down the pathway of self-revelation. Through discussion, questioning and teaching he gives those who need help the tools with which to make their own decisions. It is far more important that a person reach the right conclusion as a result of the Spirit of God working in their own heart than it is that they do the right thing. It is sometimes prudent to allow conflict to go unresolved while people examine their own heart and motives.[1]

In the end, the compassionate leader directs people into assuming personal responsibility. He promotes peace, love and truth. He protects the dignity of those involved and encourages the value of relationships. When being guided by these values a meaningful resolution can be found for every conflict. When guided by the need to win or be right, there will be nothing but pain. *"There is a way which seemeth right unto a man, but the end thereof are the ways of death. Even in laughter the heart is sorrowful; and the end of that mirth is heaviness."* Proverbs 14:12-13. No matter how sweet the illusion of victory or how loud the laughter, the need to be right ends in death.

When working with a potential leader that places a high priority on "being right" or "proving his point," I recognize the presence of a destructive character trait. I endeavor to develop a more relationship-oriented midset.

The next area of internal conflict emerges between the people and the leaders. In too many religious circles anyone who disagrees with a leader is automatically labeled as rebellious. The pat answer is always to "submit!" This ungodly philosophy has done more to breed rebellion, incite anger and promote division than almost any other in the church. Most church division starts in the pastor's heart, is proclaimed from the pulpit and enforced in the counselor's office. The more a leader tries to lead by force, the more anger and rebellion he faces. Proverbs 15:1 says that, *"Harsh, angry or contentious words stir up wrath."* The attitudes and words we sow determine the crop that grows in our organization. This is an immutable law of God.

Leaders should model humility. There are so many positive traits in humility. The least of which is by no means a teachable, approachable quality. If leaders have to always be viewed as right, it forces the people to prove they are right. It breeds fear and discourages open communication. The humble leader always gives others the right

---

[1] How to deal with those who will not resolve conflict is dealt with in another chapter.

to question. When leaders model openness, the people will follow. When leaders demonstrate a willingness to understand the grievance, people feel less driven to prove you wrong. If the leader is quick to acknowledge when he is wrong, the people are quick to forgive.

Jesus said it this way, "*Give, and it shall be given unto you; good measure, pressed down, and shaken together, and running over, shall men give into your bosom. For with the same measure that ye mete withal it shall be measured to you again.*" Luke 6:38. When we give mercy we get it back, pressed down, shaken together and running over from the people around us. Whatever we give, the people around us heap on us far greater than we gave it out. If we do not like the crop we are growing maybe it is time to plant different seeds.

When conflict between leaders and followers emerge, the senior leader must always help everyone maintain perspective. Such an occasion can provide tremendous opportunities for growth for all involved parties. The people must know they will find fairness at the top. This prevents problems from growing and festering in the pressure cooker of fear and denial. Those persons whose attitudes are not godly will want revenge and punishment for the wrong doer.

A healthy part of developing new leaders is to always remind them that people can go over their heads. Contrary to the fears of the controller, this does not encourage backbiting or gossip. It is actually a healthy deterrent. When people know they can get problems solved, they have no need to gossip or gather a delegation. Additionally, they do not hold in negative emotions toward leaders. If there are communication problems or unfairness on the part of any leader, the offended party should always have a safe place to go with their offense. Pressure that blows up does not blow out.

When solving problems between leaders and followers it is often as simple as sitting down with the leader and helping him/her understand the nature of the offense and the ministry opportunity it creates. Usually, the leader will solve the problem on their own. There should always be follow-up to the person offended and the leader to be sure it is solved. Occasionally, it may be necessary to sit in on a meeting and facilitate a healthy resolution.

The last and most difficult type of internal conflict exists between the senior leader and another member of the leadership team. Once again, this is the most essential time for us to model openness and humility. This is where we model how to be approachable. This is the place where we prove the effectiveness and conviction of our teaching. Will we live what we teach? Does the truth apply to everyone but the senior leader? Are we willing to be wrong? They will believe what our actions dictate.

As Stephen Covey points out, one of the most important laws of negotiating conflict is, "Seek to understand before seeking to be understood."[2] When I seek to be understood I am making me the focal point of the conversation. I am conveying, whether intentional or not, that I do not care about you and your feelings. I only care about my feelings. I am exalting my needs above yours, which forces you to convince me that your needs are greater than mine are.

When you believe that I want to understand your position or your need, it takes most of the fight out of the conflict. What is there to fight with? This is more than a negotiation ploy, this is the principle we should live by. Love looks first to the needs of others. I need to understand your position before I can determine the appropriate response. We pass judgement too often. We assume to know when we do not. Giving you the opportunity to be understood gives me the chance to understand and choose an appropriate response.

Obviously, not all conflicts will be resolved in a peaceful agreement. However, they can all be resolved with peace in your heart. When we walk in the law of love, there is little that can harm us. Even the most painful fire is quenched when covered with love. I have found that unresolved turmoil in my heart is always a reflection of my lack of commitment to a godly resolution. When I decide to walk in love, the grace comes to empower me and I have peace.

Conflict that is not resolved in a peaceful, productive manner lingers in the hearts of people and affects everything they do. It is a nagging burden that robs creativity and initiative. Regardless of the pain that we must face today, by dealing with this conflict, it is insignificant in comparison to the pain we will face by waiting until it festers and explodes. A wise leader is a peacemaker.

---

[2] *"Seven Habits of Highly Effective People,"* Ibid.

Questions for the heart:

1. Do I have a dread of conflict, or am I too hasty to jump into conflict?

2. What is my first response to conflict?

3. What does this tell me about my ability to peacefully resolve conflict?

4. What are my guiding principles when I attempt to resolve conflict?

5. Do I often find that I believe the one who comes first?

6. Do I have as much mercy for the wrong as for the wronged?

7. Ask people around you if they are comfortable coming to you when there is conflict to be resolved?

8. Do I try to understand first or do I insist on being understood?

9. What types of questions do I ask when attempting to convey my desire to understand?

10. Write out the value I place on peace and how that guides my conflict resolution.

NOTES

15

UNDERSTANDING BEHAVIOR

"If a man will be wise, he must know himself better than others know him. If he would be wiser still, he must know others better than they know themselves."[1] This is one of the best prescriptions for wisdom I have ever heard. When we first designed our curriculum for Impact International School of Ministry's Master's Program, we focused in on Greek, Hebrew and the deeper aspects of theological development. Following the pattern of other great schools, this seemed to be the logical pathway to higher education.

After years of working with leaders around the world, we scrapped that entire program. It is rarely theological issues that prevent effectiveness and fulfillment. Whether in the business world or the church, the number one reason for failure, strife and constant frustration is the lack of people skills. Most mediocrity emerges from ineffective people skills. Few people ever understand how their behavior effects others. Even less likely, will a person ever learn enough about the behavior of others to have effective communication. We all want the rest of the world to conform to our standards and opinions. If everyone else would change, everything would be alright.

The development of effective people skills begins by understanding our own behavior. Only when you understand your behavior will you understand your reactions and influence on others. So often someone will say, "People always accuse me of ___!" Or, "Everybody thinks that I ____!" "People have always said that ____!" This is the classic, "I get tired of everyone saying ____!" What is the common denominator in each of these scenarios? You!

Just because people perceive something to be true about you does not make it true. It does mean that there is something in your behavior that leads people to believe it is true. Whether it is true or not is not the issue. The issue is whether it is perceived or not. If people perceive something to be true they will relate to you accordingly. As unfair as this may seem, we must assume responsibility

---

[1] I would love to take credit for this statement, but the source is actually unknown.

for our actions. If we want everyone to relate to us differently, we can wait for everyone else to change or we can change. Since I do not have the right to demand change of anyone else, that only leaves me.

You do not really have to change who you are. Actually, you must come to understand what is motivating your behavior and decide if you like the outcome. If you do not like what your behavior is producing in any situation, you do not have to change your whole life; you simply have to change how you express yourself in that environment. The inflexible leader says; "I am the boss. I do not have to change!" The effective leader says; "I will stay true to my beliefs and values, but I will change my methods of expression and communication to be more effective."

One of the greatest changes in my life happened when I came to understand my behavior and how others perceived it.[2] This brought more positive change in my relationships and reduced conflict more than anything that ever happened to me. When I got saved, I changed morally. Relationally, I was still pretty much a jerk. I was saved, but I was just a saved jerk. Only after learning about my own behavior was I able to begin to understand the behavior of others. Thus, I began to understand what people really wanted when they asked certain kinds of questions. I was set free from judgement and empowered to walk in love more than ever before in my life.

One of the greatest sources of judgement comes when we use ourselves as the standard of reason. We think that others do things for the same reason we do things. This is judging. It is forbidden of God, yet, it is how most of us live our lives. For example, if you are an indirect person, you probably only speak very direct when you are angry. Therefore, when anyone speaks to you in a direct manner, you assume they are angry. That is a judgement, using yourself as the standard of reason.

If you are uncomfortable with physical contact, you reserve physical contact only when there is love or lust. When you see someone, especially of the opposite sex, making physical contact, you assume they are sending a sexual signal. You think they do things for the same reason you do them. Unless that person is just like you,

---

[2] For more information about Behavioral Seminars or other training tools contact Impact Ministries.

they never do things for your reasons; they do them for their reasons. It is this false perception, based on personal judgement, that causes us to respond to people in ways that seem completely irrational.

This information brought me to a tremendous realization. When I want to know why someone is doing something, ask. Do not judge! Too often, I have assumed to know why someone does something only to find, after the damage was done, that I was completely wrong. The mind always seeks equilibrium. It always seeks to prove what it believes. When we pass a judgement, we enter a process of selective reasoning. We begin to exclude from our mind anything that would disprove our position. Conversely, we only notice those things that validate our position. We become like the Pharisees who were blinded by their sin because they insisted they could see! My insistence that I see things as they are is what blinds me to the way things really are. If I decide who you are I can never know the real you. My perception becomes limited to my judgement.

Understanding the behavior of another empowers me to walk in love. It matters not what truth I possess. If I do not walk in love, it does not benefit you or me.[3] To walk in love I must consider you. I can do that most effectively if I understand your behavior. If you are uncomfortable with direct, bottom line communication, I should respect that and communicate with you in a less direct manner. This prevents discomfort for you and increases the overall effectiveness of our communication.

The self-centered leader is quick to respond, "Why do they not just grow up? Do I have to change for them?" Are you saying everyone but you should change so you will be comfortable? Who is really being self-centered here? Loving leaders model their willingness to yield and stretch beyond their comfort zone for the benefit of others. This does not mean you change who you are. This is not manipulation or deceit; this is courtesy. This is preferring others above ourselves! Romans 12:10 says, "*Be kindly affectioned one to another with brotherly love; in honour preferring one another.*" The leader who honors others does not ask others to make him comfortable; he seeks to make them comfortable.

Nothing will give you more tools to effectively

---

[3] I Corinthians 13:1-13

minister the gospel than a clear understanding of yourself and others.[4] When communicating, there are some who want more details, some who want more inspiration; and there are others who want to experience power. This is why there were four gospels written in four different ways. Even God was smart enough to record the life of the Savior in as many ways as it took to be effective with the different perceptions.

There are four basic behavioral styles that group together to make up over 100 behavior patterns. A speaker who uses only one style runs the risk of excluding 75% of the listeners. Any communicator who does what is personally comfortable alienates the greatest number of people. The loving leader assumes the responsibility to understand others better than they understand themselves. His desire to be effective supercedes the desire to be comfortable.

Motivation is an important tool for the nurturing leader. He recognizes that people are motivated by different environments. One person benefits from the pep-rally environment. Another behavior type is completely turned off by what they perceive as hype. One behavior needs a shock, a reality check. For another that would be the last straw; that would feel like pressure and manipulation. A true motivator understands that motivation is an internal virtue. He realizes that he need only create the right environment and the individual will motivate himself.

Everything we do with others becomes more effective when we perceive and respond to their needs in a way that is most positive for them. A well-orchestrated reward can become an insult if presented in a way that is offensive for that particular individual. A minor correction can erupt into a volcanic explosion just by approaching it the wrong way. The Bible says, *"A word fitly spoken is like apples of gold in pictures of silver."* Proverbs 25:11. It is not enough that our words be apples of gold. They must be served in an attractive setting. This only comes when we are responsive to the behavioral tendencies of others.

It is essential that our leadership team develop the very best behavioral skills. We are all in the people business. Not one dollar can be made in business, not one soul can be helped; nothing of consequence can happen in this earth apart from effective communication.

---

[4] Impact International School of Ministry's Master's Program will be complete in 1999. Call for details.

Questions for the heart:

1. Am I often surprised at what people say about me?

2. What is the main remark that I disagree with?

3. What is there in my behavior that makes this believable?

4. What type of person do I usually have conflict with?

5. What do I understand about that person's behavioral style?

6. Do I think others should change to make me more comfortable?

7. Why?

8. Do I feel manipulative if I change my communication style with an individual?

9. Is there a particular person that I cannot motivate or lead?

10. What priority have I placed on developing my people skills?

11. What would change in my organization if a higher emphasis was placed on developing people skills in our leadership team?

16

BECOMING A FACILITATOR

In the early years I was often frustrated with Jesus' teaching style. I wondered why He did not make things clearer. So many times He could have just come out with a straight answer and it seemed it would have settled the problem. Fortunately, I held fast my commitment to the fact that God's ways were always effective and I sought to understand that which violated my opinion. As time went by, I recognized the frailty of the teaching methods employed in twentieth-century Christianity. Yet, I could not recognize the subtle, yet essential differences between the Biblical pattern and our cultural trends.

After years of ministry I have come to realize that people need to experience the personal process of self-discovery. By self-discovery I mean that people need to grow in God and experience the Holy Spirit as their personal teacher. They need to discover the revelation and power of God for themselves. They do not need to develop into my disciple. The believer should never become dependent on the leader. They need to become a disciple of Jesus. They need to learn the internal process of transformation.[1]

With all of our talk about the Holy Spirit in the last twenty years, we have continued to move farther and farther away from Him and His ministry in the believer. The teaching revolution gave rise to people who, instead of teaching the Word of God and allowing the believer to seek and experience God for himself, taught their experiences. The believer, instead of seeking to commune with and experience God, began to seek a duplicate experience. The end result has been people mimicking the experiences of others instead of allowing the Spirit of God to lead us into whatever truth and experience would be relevant to our situation.

Through our attempts to take people through the process of transformation we have emphasized the need for information to such a degree that few people really experi-

---

[1] Look for an upcoming release by Dr. Richards entitled, "*How to Bring About Permanent, Painless Change Without Effort.*" To be released in 1999.

ence Spirit-empowered transformation. The focus is on what the leader can do for the person rather than what God can do for them. The result is a house full of converts who look to the leader to do what only God can do. I have often preached in churches where the congregation looked and acted like the pastor. This will always happen to some degree, but when we think that our leader is the model and we are trying to become like him, we are focusing on the wrong person.

Our concept of leadership is more like pushing, dragging or forcing. We teach like an overprotective mother that gasps every time the child attempts to take a step, thus paralyzing the child with the fear of failure. We attempt to motivate by fear. We withhold love and affection in an attempt to force someone in the right direction. We try to bring about change as if it is something that comes from the outside and works its way to the inside. There is little in our twentieth century methods of ministry and leadership that closely resembles the methods Jesus employed.

As we develop our team we must model the role of a leader as a facilitator. A facilitator knows where the follower must go, but he recognizes and respects the person and trusts the Spirit of God in the person enough to allow change to be a personal and individual experience. A facilitator does not play God. He does just what the word implies; he facilitates the opportunity for growth. He allows the person to walk at whatever pace he is walking. He respects that each person must process truth for himself.

As a leader it is not my job to bring change. It is my job to create a safe environment that is conducive to transformation. It is my job to provide the tools that one would need for transformation. It is my job to nurture and encourage. It is my job to convey love and acceptance. Whatever changes you desire must be your choice. They must be the product of your own search for God. It is never my job to change you.

An effective leader develops recognition for the difference between change and transformation. Change is the process whereby we attempt to become that which we are not. The attempt to bring change denies everything the Bible teaches about the new birth. It denies that we are in fact made righteous by the finished work of Jesus. It denies that we are holy, sanctified and full of power.

Change becomes something we seek as a means to earn those things from God. It is a vain attempt through the observance of rules and the modifying of behavior to accomplish that which can only be accomplished in the heart by the power God.

Transformation, on the other hand, is a metamorphosis that comes as we yield to the righteousness of God that is in us. Transformation comes as one yields to the truth. Transformation is the result of believing "I am" not I am becoming. Transformation is dependence upon an internal reality. If I believe I am a new creation in Christ,[2] then I am not seeking to change. I am seeking to allow that which is in me to arise.

The facilitator learns the art of asking questions. He is a great listener. Proverbs says, "*Counsel in the heart of man is like deep water; but a man of understanding will draw it out.*" Proverbs 20:5. Proverbs also says that a foolish person delights in airing his opinions. He loves to be heard. The immature leader finds more joy in providing the answer than facilitating the person's discovery of the answer.

As we develop the leaders around us we are tempted to provide all the answers. They often have the answers, but because of fear of being wrong they defer to us. We mistakenly begin to think they know nothing, thus treating them as if they know nothing. We unwittingly paralyze personal growth and individual decision-making. Before we give an answer, it may be wise to always ask how they would handle the situation, or what they think. Give them the opportunity to confirm their ability to make decisions. So often, when I ask a person what they think they should do, they have the right answer. They need to experience hearing the wisdom of God in their own heart. I then validate their ability to make wise decisions.

When a member of our leadership team presents an unacceptable solution, it is important that they learn the process of making sound decisions. Ask questions that lead them through the process. Teach them to brainstorm. Nudge them into independent thought. As they grasp the

---

[2] "*The Prayer Organizer,*" James B. Richards, Impact International Publishing, Huntsville, Alabama. "*The Prayer Organizer*" is a system of prayer that focuses completely on the finished work of Jesus and our new identity in Him. It is designed to facilitate transformation while establishing a Bible-based sense of identity, self-image and self-worth.

logic of decision-making they will make good decisions in the future. Additionally, they will understand your logic and become a better team player.

It has been said that the person who will influence your life the most is not the person you believe in; it is the person who believes in you.[3] The egocentric leader wants his followers to believe in him. He mistakenly believes that if his followers elevate him to a place of honor in their own mind, it will be to their benefit. The enlightened leader recognizes the need to convey his confidence in his leadership team. He recognizes that a man of honor is in fact a man that bestows honor on others. By expressing our confidence in our leaders, we facilitate growth, confidence and initiative.

As we allow the freedom of personal development to continue in our leadership team they will extend that freedom to the people they serve. The end result is stability. This is the true process of making disciples unto the Lord Jesus. There is, however, little room for vainglory in this process. We are, after all, only vessels. It is the treasure in this vessel that gives it its worth. A leader who facilitates growth is satisfied when the student functions successfully, independent of his intervention. We do, after all, raise our children to become adults, not large children. Let us develop our staff to be leaders.

---

[3] Source Unknown.

Questions for the heart:

1. Read some Gospel accounts of Jesus teaching or being asked for counsel. Make note of the differences between His approach and what your approach would be.

2. How would you describe the Holy Spirit's ministry to the believer?

3. Make a list of ways that you feel you infringe on that ministry.

4. Do I feel responsible for the growth of others?

5. How do I feel when someone is not progressing at my desired pace?

6. When people come to me for advice, do I usually begin by asking questions or making statements?

7. For one week make it a point to ask more questions than to make statements. Record the interesting experiences.

8. Create a situation with a small group of people, i.e., staff meeting, cell group, where you facilitate others in their discussion without becoming the center of the discussion. Tactfully refuse to be drawn into the center.

9. Write out the positive and negative feelings you had from the previous experience and how you evaluate those emotions.

10. Make a list of what you can do to help others feel that you believe in them.

17

HIRING AND FIRING

Ted Nicholas points out in his course *Magic Words* that a leader should be slow to hire and quick to fire. At first glance this seems a little cruel, but it is not nearly as cruel as hiring too fast and waiting too long to fire. The latter promotes much more pain and suffering. The impatient leader always hires too quickly. The need to gratify his impulsiveness forces him to justify swift, often premature, decision-making. This is an injustice to the organization, the current staff and the new employee.

The leader who hires too quickly will always regret it. Some organizations do not have the opportunity to observe a person in a non-paid role before hiring them. In such cases, find out all you can. Too often the hyper-spiritual leader says, "I feel good about this person," and that is supposed to justify a professional decision that will affect this person's livelihood and the stability of your organization. Hardly! Even if I have a good track record for making decisions in this manner, it is always safe to confirm with hard evidence before making a commitment. We are dealing with people's lives. They should be handled with care.

In a ministry situation you should know all you can about a person before making them a part of your ministry team. You should have a Behavioral Profile[1] that helps you understand how this person relates to others. How are they motivated and de-motivated? How do they respond to stress? How do they communicate? How flexible and adaptable are they? How do they respond to aggression? What do they consider to be aggression? How do they change when they are under pressure? This is essential information. This information is rarely a determining factor when I hire someone, but it does give me insight into how I can effectively lead them.

We have found that it can be a great value to keep detailed profiles[2] of all staff members available for other

---

[1] The D-I-S-C Behavioral Profile is a product of Performax Systems, Minneapolis, Minnesota, and are available through Impact International Publications.

[2] A detailed profile is a computer generated profile, based on the D-I-S-C model, that provides all of this information and more.

staff members to review at any time. This information becomes a valuable resource to avoid potential conflict or to solve emerging conflict.[3] Because we place such a premium on communication and transparency, a potential staff member who is uncomfortable with this type of self-revelation would never be comfortable on my team.

It is equally important that a potential staff member know all he/she can about each of the current team members, especially the senior leader. I want this person to read my profile. I want to spend time talking with them. I want them to ask me all of their tough questions. I encourage all new team members to talk to other staff members in private. Ask them what it is like to work for me. Let the other team members openly discuss what they like and what they do not like about working for me. I do not want surprises for me or for a new staff member. If you are joining my team I want us both to know all we can about one another.

Too often, we hire like we date. In dating we are afraid to let the potential spouse see any of our negative traits. We are afraid they will no longer desire us. The real pain comes, however, when we get married and they discover all of those traits and it destroys the relationship. I want you to know the good and bad of working for me, before we "get married." If you do not think you can work for me, we can still maintain a positive relationship. If you come to work and it blows up, it will be challenging to work through those negatives.

I also recommend checking a person's employment record, their credit record and every other available bit of information. None of these single bits of information would qualify or disqualify a person, unless it is a moral or ethical problem. What I am looking for are trends more than individual events. As mentioned in a previous chapter people seldom understand how their behavior is affecting the people around them. A repeated conflict of the same nature reflects a high level of self-centeredness or a failure to understand one's self. I may want the opportunity to discuss this before we proceed, especially if it will effect your ability to function in your area of responsibility.

As you have probably figured, the length of time involved in bringing a person onto your team could be

---

[3] To receive a detailed profile on all of your staff, contact Impact Ministries.

quite long. There is a natural safety in hiring slow. Many mistakes are made out of expediency. This process keeps me from hiring just because I have a need. It also keeps a desperate person who simply needs a job from pursuing our team as a mere source of employment. I do not want people who are looking for a job. I want people who have a sense of destiny, call and purpose. Good teams are built around longevity, relationship and personal commitment. But it takes time to build this kind of team!

We have another important factor in our team building process. It is called "justified income." Justified income is an essential business and spiritual factor. The church world is filled with "hirelings." A hireling is a person who is just there for the money. I believe people should be paid as well as your resources will allow. But I have zero tolerance for the hireling. The hireling just has a job. He/she will be gone when there are any hardships. Their commitment is to earning a living, not serving others.

When I pioneered my church I had no guaranteed income. Actually, I had to take money from my own pocket to get it started. I supported myself from my own resources. As the church grew, we first paid the overhead. Later, we began to buy chairs and other essential pieces of equipment. Eventually, I began to receive expense money and finally a salary. For every independent church that starts, someone has to go through this process. Someone makes sacrifices and commitments to get it going. This person has a vested interest.

There are some staff positions that immediately provide the opportunity for income. Most of them must be developed. Many times a person has to start out as non-paid staff to develop that area, or we have to borrow money from another area. Ultimately, that area of ministry must create its own finances. It must create the finances to pay its overhead, a staff member and contribute to the local church. If this does not happen, the church must value it enough to make special contributions. In short, any paid staff position must directly create income to justify its existence, or it must give freedom to an existing staff member to create additional finances.[4]

---

[4] Additionally, each new position must be a part of contributing to the quality of ministry we offer. This has been covered in previous chapters.

By hiring slow, you seldom have surprises. When problems arise they must be addressed quickly, especially if you see patterns emerge. Individual incidents could reflect a misunderstanding or an oversight. Patterns usually reflect a lifestyle. When approaching a person about a problem, you must never judge. In other words, you do not know why they did what they did, you may not even be sure you have the accurate facts. Always allow a person to tell their version of a problem, but always let that person know that you will talk to everyone involved. There is no secret reporting. Do not say privately what you are not willing to say openly.

Because we maintain openness we never have secret information. We seldom ever have staff members who desire to "get" another team member. There is a high level of trust in this safe environment. If someone reports a problem, they need to be ready, in love and kindness, to address the situation and the people involved. It is rare that someone comes to me about a problem with a coworker. We have established a pattern of honest conflict resolution. The staff usually settles their difference without my involvement. When your team believes you are fair and equitable they rarely try to hide or manipulate the facts. You will encounter an amazing level of honesty.

When assessing a situation or a problem with a staff member, I must ask myself if this problem is a problem of selfishness or insensitivity. Is this a single act or is there a pattern emerging? Does this violate our most essential principles? As previously mentioned, I will not allow a person to take advantage of the people they serve. We are here to serve, not use. I also want to know if this is a problem that will affect the overall peace of the organization. Whatever the seriousness of the problem I will seek to protect everyone involved. I will always seek to restore the offender, even if I must dismiss them.

When adding a new staff member, I always let them know that they will be dismissed for creating strife or taking advantage of people. Almost anything else has the potential to be worked through. When people need personal help we provide counseling and encouragement. We provide a strong support system for those who need and desire help. However, not all problems can be helped while the person is still on staff. Because of the way we have handled it, we have often had staff members who were released and remain a healthy part of our congrega-

NOTES

134

tion. Some have eventually returned to a staff position.

If I believe you are the right person for the job, I do not give up on you just because it is not working at this moment. The fact that we maintain a high level of ongoing relationship with past staff members is a positive sign about the way we handle these difficult situations. The guiding rule for confrontation is this, "Never touch a person's self-worth." Once we touch a person's self-worth, all meaningful communication is over. Regardless of the violation, that person is still a child of God and they are still important. They have now stepped into the realm of the one needing ministry instead of the one giving ministry.

Once you realize this situation is not working, it is essential that you communicate that and your intentions to the staff member. Too many times, motivated by our own needs, we are afraid to be honest with a staff member when the situation is not working out acceptably. I have had a few situations that were so potentially disastrous that I had to send the person home at that moment. Usually, however, it is a positive process of reassuring, encouraging and validating. I have had people that I informed they would be let go and we have spent months working it through in such a way that did not hurt their self-worth or their finances. We must work through every negative situation in a way that is best for everyone.

If you hire slow, it is seldom that a person is dismissed for character problems. Usually, it simply is not working. That does not mean that person could not be productive elsewhere. As a matter of fact, I have often sat down with a person and said, "It is not working here, but I think you could be effective in another area. Your skills and talents would be more effective here!" We have often moved people to another area of our ministry.

Because people so closely associate their self-worth and their work performance, this should be handled with the greatest of care. We should be honest about why it is not working. When possible, we should point out their strengths. If we are offering them options, we should make those options clear. Then, give them time to think them through. Clearly describe how long you plan to take in walking them through the process of removal. If a person has been a faithful staff member, be as generous as your resources will allow. The church has a bad reputation for using people as long as they are an asset and throwing

NOTES

135

them away when they are no longer "usable."

A compassionate leader recognizes that there will be times when people encounter situations that effect their life so dramatically that their personal performance drops terribly. This is when we must be willing to suffer loss. The last thing a person needs is another hardship. When someone loses a loved one, has family conflict or health problems, their work will usually suffer. These are not grounds for dismissal. If they continue over a long period of time with the person attempting to get help, the situation could change. Many times, we have kept staff members far past their ability to be productive. We had to suffer loss for the sake of someone who had been faithful in the past. We must never forget our staff members are also our church members.

There will also be times when a current, valuable staff member wants to leave. In an open, positive team relationship, that person should feel the freedom to express that desire openly, without fear of retribution. We never know what God has planned for a person. We do not know the will of God for anyone. They must walk through that process with complete peace. When there is an open environment the dissatisfied team member can discuss their desire to leave. It may be that he/she wants to do something else, or it could be something in the present environment is de-motivating or stressful? Where people communicate honestly without fear you can often move the person internally. Many times a sacrificial leader can recover a good staff member by listening and offering options. If there is no internal option that seems appealing, we should become a part of helping them make a positive decision for relocation. I have spent up to a year helping a person prepare to leave. But that person helped me prepare to bring in another person. Instead of leaving on bad terms these people leave as ambassadors for our ministry.

We believe in the motto, "Hire slow and fire fast." When it comes to firing fast, I view that more as communicating your intention "fast." If it is not working, do not wait until you are frustrated to communicate. Quickly find a way to get it working or find a peaceful way to process that person out of the team. Keep them as friends when possible. Become a positive force in helping them relocate. But never try to make an unworkable situation workable. Likewise, never insist that you know the will of God for that person. Allow them to walk out their decisions in their own maturity and integrity. Otherwise, more people will be hurt. It is merely prolonged agony! When they want to leave, let them go.

Hire and fire with integrity. Never lose sight of the fact that you are dealing with people and their resources.

Questions for the heart:

1. What is my process for hiring?

2. What could I change to make this process more effective?

3. What do I do to learn all I can about a potential staff member?

4. What do I do to make sure they know all they can about me?

5. When a staff member is not working out, do I procrastinate, discuss the problem, offer options or just fire them?

6. Do I maintain positive relationships with previous staff members?

7. What is the worst experience I have ever had with a staff member?

8. In light of what you now know, how could that have been handled?

9. What is my reaction when a staff member wants to leave?

10. How many staff members have I helped to relocate?

18

GIVING HONOR

Romans 13:7 says, *"Render...honour to whom honour is due."* There are many ways of showing honor. Regardless of the method you choose it is important that we show honor when it is due. Every organization must have some system of reward, recognition and honor. Some would think that reward is vanity, but it is actually a vital part of the emotional make-up of human beings. The Bible is full of stories of godly people who were motivated, in part, by the reward. Even Jesus was motivated by the reward. *"Looking unto Jesus the author and finisher of our faith; who for the joy that was set before him endured the cross, despising the shame, and is set down at the right hand of the throne of God."* Hebrews 12:2. David was motivated to face Goliath for the reward offered by the king.

It is important that we understand the behavior pattern of the person we honor. Different people benefit by receiving honor in different ways. If our efforts are for the benefit of the one we seek to honor, it would be good to do it in a way that benefits them the most. One of the first ways to honor a person is through their pay. Pay as generously as possible, within the limits of your resources. If your resources are limited, always let the people know they are worth more. Assure them that they ·will be rewarded financially when it is possible.

For most people, emotional support is as important as financial support. Do the things that promote emotional self-respect. Never take credit for the work of others. Always acknowledge the efforts and accomplishments of others. As a senior leader I recognize that I have no isolated victories. Everything I accomplish is the result of a team effort. Every person on my team should share in the same sense of accomplishment. When people receive the emotional support and recognition they deserve they will bond with the leader and the organization

Never demand honor. In our twisted society, some teach that leaders should demand a certain type of treatment. I once knew a pastor who discovered that his church was not having a birthday party for him. He demanded they have a party. After all, he reasoned, they should honor their pastor. I cannot imagine such childishness in a minister. Yet, it is rampant in some of the areas of the twentieth century church. The established leader has his own sense of honor that comes from internal resources. He is not looking to others to meet that need. Instead, he is looking for the opportunity to give honor to others.

Proverbs 20:3 says, *"It is an honour for a man to cease from strife: but every fool will be meddling."* A man of honor does not enter into strife and quarreling, especially striving to make another person show him honor. Proverbs 12:16 goes on to say, *"A fool shows his annoyance at once, but a prudent man overlooks an insult."* NIV. A wise man who has honor overlooks an insult. A fool who wants people to perceive him as having honor demands that no one insult him. It is not, however, the absence of insult that proves we are people with honor. It is the fact that we do not receive the insult and enter into strife that proves we have a sense of personal honor. The very fact that we demand to be treated as special reveals our lack of confidence and egocentric motivation.

Honor is not something others give me. It is something I have. If I have honor I show honor. In many organizations they have classes that teach the members how to show honor to the pastors. I wholeheartedly agree that people should show honor to leaders. However, if you are the one making the sacrifice, you are the one with honor; not the one to whom you extend honorable treatment! It should be taught that showing honor is a reflection of your own honor, not the honor of the one you serve. Showing honor is something you do because of who you are, not who the other person is.

As the senior leader, if I have honor, I can always extend that honor to the other leaders. Honor flows from the top down, not from the bottom up. I do not give honor by placing a person on a man-made pedestal. I give honor as an expression of my personal sense of dignity. As the leaders around me experience the fruit of my character, they will walk in what I have modeled. When they extend courtesy and patience, when they give rewards or other acts of kindness and gratitude, they are expressing their personal sense of honor. When others experience the fruit of their character, they will seek to develop the same character. If everyone in the organization is a servant, no one will lack. If everyone has honor, all will give honor.

A leader who does not give honor is a person who

has no personal sense of honor. Likewise, a person who cannot receive honor lacks a personal sense of honor. The person who demands honor usually has a low sense of self-worth that is expressing itself through pride and control. A leader must have a sense of God-centered dignity and worth. How I feel about me must be derived from how God feels about me. Otherwise, I will pressure people to give me what can only be found in God.

The Bible teaches that God crowned man with dignity and worth.[1] It was a part of our essential emotional make-up. Man cannot live a healthy, normal life apart from the sense of dignity and worth. The godly leader recognizes this need and has true value for every human being. He recognizes that Jesus died for the sins of the world, not the sins of those who are doing right. From the realization of God's value for man, he has great value for man. The spiritual leader recognizes that the truth only helps when it nurtures a healthy sense of God-centered self-worth. The leader who does not value all man-kind lacks value for what God did through the Lord Jesus.

All of the principles or practices presented in this book will only have value when their application is governed by a heartfelt love for God and man. Apart from the motivation of love, all the practices of man eventually erode to a self-centered attempt to control for personal gain. This must be the heart of the leader and this must be the heart of the team. Even the most archaic attempts at leadership will have a measurable success when love and respect motivate the actions.

The compassionate leader has great value for all men, saints or sinners, dark skinned or light skinned, kind or cruel. He recognizes the value that God expressed through the finished work of Jesus and he attempts to be an expression of that value. The leader who has no value for man uses others to give him a sense of personal value while stripping others of their value. In the end, a leader with honor instills honor in all to whom he has exposure. When surrounded by people of honor and integrity, no task is impossible.

---

[1] *"Dignity and Worth,"* James B. Richards, Impact International Publications, Huntsville, Alabama

Question for the heart:

1. Do I insist that others treat me special?

2. What efforts do I put forth to make others feel special?

3. What are some ways I can reward people around me?

4. Write down each staff/team member and make a note of how that person best receives appreciation.

5. How do I really feel about people in general?
   A. Do I have more value for those who live right?
   B. Do I only express value to those who benefit me or my ministry?

6. Do people around me strive for my approval?

7. How do I really feel about myself?

8. How does that affect the people around me?

9. Am I hyper-sensitive to insult? What does that reflect about me?

10. Would I be comfortable with a leader like me?

LEADERSHIP PROVERBS

These thirty leadership proverbs should be read daily. There is one for each day of the month. I would recommend reading them for several months. Unlike the chapters of this book they have no questions for you to answer. As you read these proverbs and the brief comments, ponder them in your heart. Write out the questions that arise in your mind about your personal leadership and about the leadership team that you seek to develop.

Day 1

"Withhold no good from them to whom it is due, when it is in the power of thine hand to do it." Proverbs 3:27.

Promotion, when properly used, is a very powerful incentive! When improperly used it can be a source of frustration and discouragement. The desire to grow, expand and succeed is a part of the basic make-up of the human race. A wise leader handles the power of promotion with the greatest of respect. The negative leader sees everything people do wrong and seldom finds the opportunity to promote. Someone has said, "A leader looks for opportunities to find someone doing something right." I say to go a step beyond; look for opportunities to promote.

Failure to promote those who deserve it produces discouragement and frustration. Promotion of those who do not deserve it is even more destructive. Mark Twain said, "It is better to deserve honors and not have them than to have them and not deserve them." Promotion of an unworthy person is a testimony to the foolishness of a leader. Never pass over a person who deserves a promotion and never promote a person who does not deserve it.

Promotion can never be the product of friendship or favoritism. There must be a clearly established process of promotion that reflects a person's accomplishments. People should only be promoted when they have been proven. The Bible teaches that depending on an unfaithful servant (employee/staff member) is like chewing on a broken tooth or standing on a foot out of joint (Proverbs 25:19). If they are promoted without being proven, in the time of trouble, you will be the one in trouble.

Too often, promotion is given to the person who knows how to promote or sell himself. He may not be better at his job, but he may be better at drawing attention to his job. Often, the hardest workers and the most valued employees are overlooked simply because they are not competent at selling themselves. Do we want to promote those who are great at selling themselves or do we want to promote those who are competent at their job?

Day 2

"He that laboureth laboureth for himself; for his mouth craveth it of him." Proverbs 16:26

People do things for their own reasons, not your reasons. If their reasons are inconsistent with yours, they should not be a member of your leadership team. It is essential that every leader have a sense of fulfilling their personal goals. He/she must have the sense that they are fulfilling their own ministry, not just ours. As such, they manage themselves as one who is self-employed and will be internally motivated. An internally motivated person requires a minimum amount of external motivation.

If you must continually motivate a person to do their job, there is a definite problem. Cyrus Curtis said, "There are two kinds of men who never amount to much: those who cannot do what they are told, and those who can do nothing else." Excessive oversight is a burden on the employee, the leader and the organization. Those who will become effective leaders usually need a minimum amount of "management." Someone has said, "It's the person who doesn't need a boss that's usually selected to be one."[1]

While there could be several different situations that require excessive management and motivation, we will focus on the two. Either they have a poor work ethic or they are not doing what brings them fulfillment. If they are not doing what they want to do, they will always be a weak link in the team. They will be the "bottleneck," and they will always require external motivation.

When motivation is external it can easily become manipulation. Motivation is when we remind a person of their dreams and they motivate themselves. Manipulation is when we attempt to excite a person to do what we want them to do. This type of effort must be continually repeated. It is not the true desire of the person.

If this person is a good team member, it is essential that he/she be relocated to a task that is performed from

---

[1] Source unknown

internal motivation. A quality person with a passion will always be productive when placed in the right position.

Day 3

"Delight is not seemly for a fool; much less for a servant to have rule over princes." Proverbs 19:10

A worker does not necessarily make a good leader. Yet, the system we have created tends to exalt leaders and diminish workers. Because leaders are usually the mouth-piece of the organization we exalt the position of leader-ship as a way to make ourselves secure. In so doing, we minimize the role of the worker, the helper and the giver. The honor we give leaders forces every person to aspire to a leadership position.

We should give honor, recognition and appreciation for every person who is a part of our team. Every person should have a sense of fulfillment from the task they perform. No position should be elevated above the other. Every person should see how his or her part is essential to the accomplishment of the whole.

Good servants should never be promoted to a position of leadership as a means to feel good about his task. Likewise, leaders should never be made to feel they are above the workers. Every team member should have a sense of honor and fulfillment from their part of a task.

Day 4

"Train up a child in the way he should go: and when he is old, he will not depart from it." Proverbs 22:6

The Amplified Bible translates this as raising a child according to his particular "bent." Whether a child or an employee, it is best to allow a person to follow their particular "bent." When people are allowed the opportunity to do what they enjoy, they will excel with little effort. Harvey Mackey said, "Find something you love to do and you will never have to work another day in your life."

When people attempt to function too long outside of their comfort zone they begin to experience "perceptional stress." Perceptional stress is created by the perception of the situation. For example, one person would look forward to resolving an existing conflict. They would view it as an opportunity to bring resolution. Another person would dread and fear conflict resolution. In their mind it would be a pathway to more conflict and pain. Or, one person would find deep fulfillment from nurturing and comforting a person who is down. Another person would have negative feelings about the same endeavor. They would perceive the need to be encouraged as a weakness.

Some people prefer verbal communication; some like written. Some flourish with a variety of tasks, others enjoy becoming specialists at one task. Always develop a leader in places where they will flourish. Stick with their particular "bent."

While we all need situations that stretch us beyond our comfort zones, it is not wise to attempt to work outside of our particular "bent" everyday. Stretching is done gradually and in consumable doses. It is even more disastrous to place a person in a leadership role that feels uncomfortable leading others in the area that is out of their personal "bent." If a leader feels uncomfortable in a particular role, he will send subtle, unintended messages to the follower, creating discomfort and sometimes chaos.

Occasionally, everyone must perform a task that stretches them beyond the limits of their comfort zone. However, it is usually best to find someone who enjoys the task. They will help the followers to enjoy it as well.

Day 5

"Cast out the scorner, and contention shall go out; yea, strife and reproach shall cease." Proverbs 22:10

Of all that we refuse to tolerate, at the top of the list should be those who create conflict. Conflict and disagreement are not the same. The leader who does not allow disagreement will force conflict, gossip and strife. If we allow people to vent up, they do not vent out.

If we have created an environment that is conducive to resolving conflict, mature people will always seek healthy resolution. When one does not go through the proper channels to resolve conflict in a positive setting, it is either a character flaw or a desire to create strife. Neither of which can be allowed in our leaders.

If it is a character flaw, then the individual must be developed. Many times, leaders who have mishandled a situation have gone on to develop powerful skills in the very area of their weakness. If, however, it is a deliberate attempt to cause conflict the person must be dismissed. When people deliberately cause conflict, they are always working some larger agenda. There is always something they seek to gain from the conflict. When they are willing to hurt the people and the organization for personal gain they cannot be tolerated.

It has always been my experience that those who complain and create strife in the pursuit of personal gain always do it again. "A complaining spirit is first a caller, then a guest, and finally a master."[2] Once entrapped, few ever escape the grip of this tormenting master.

Day 6

"Righteousness exalteth a nation: but sin is a reproach to any people." Proverbs 13:34

Leadership requires the acceptance of more responsibility, not more privilege. The leader who feels he has more privilege will lead others astray. People follow the course of the leader, plus a little. The follower always goes slightly beyond the bounds of the leader.

Every person is given the gift of righteousness when they are born again. A wise leader inspires people to walk in their new nature. The path of righteousness is not the path of legalism and dead works. It is a wide, open place of rest, healing and strength. The Bible tells us to, *"Ponder the path of thy feet, and let all thy ways be established. Turn not to the right hand nor to the left: remove thy foot from evil."* Proverbs 4:26-27.

Although we have been made righteous, we can walk in any path we choose. Where we walk determines what we experience. God has bought us every good thing through the death, burial and resurrection of Jesus. If we choose to walk in the pathway of destruction, we will experience destruction. God walks in paths of righteousness. If we are to walk with God, we must walk where He is walking.

The loving leader desires to see his people receive all that Jesus died to give. He leads his people in the paths of righteousness. He facilitates the opportunity for them to experience the very best God has to give. He does not view sin as something he must condemn and punish. He views it as a pathway to pain and suffering.

---

[2] Source unknown

Day 7

"He that reproveth a scorner getteth to himself shame: and he that rebuketh a wicked man getteth himself a blot. Reprove not a scorner, lest he hate thee: rebuke a wise man, and he will love thee. Give instruction to a wise man, and he will be yet wiser: teach a just man, and he will increase in learning." Proverbs 9:7-9

The Word of God is filled with many principles of communication. The wise leader learns and abides by these principles. It is in the act of communication that we most often create personal and organizational difficulties. *"For in many things we offend all. If any man offend not in word, the same is a perfect man, and able also to bridle the whole body."* James 3:2.

The wise leader recognizes the one who will receive instruction and correction. Likewise, he recognizes who will not. It is vanity to correct or instruct a scorner. The words of instruction will be twisted and you will find no peace. *"If a wise man contendeth with a foolish man, whether he rage or laugh, there is no rest."* Proverbs 29:9.

To have peace, develop leaders who instruct those who demonstrate a willingness to grow and learn. Leave those alone who prove themselves to be unteachable and argumentative. A foolish person will only learn by consequences. They will not learn by instruction. When the wise contend with a fool, they actually disrupt the only process whereby a fool can learn, i.e., consequences.

Day 8

"The integrity of the upright shall guide them: but the perverseness of transgressors shall destroy them." Proverbs 11:3

In the absence of instruction people are led by their heart. If their heart is committed to righteousness they will always discover the righteous path. If their heart is full of unrighteousness, they will find that path. A person may momentarily rise above or sink beneath the level of integrity in their heart, but they always return to what is truly in their heart.

A wise leader always gives the workers a degree of freedom - not enough freedom to self-destruct, nor enough freedom to damage the organization. He does, however, provide enough freedom for the person to expose his level of character. The fair leader does not judge. He observes. When one habitually abuses freedom, we may not know what the motivation of the heart is, but we do know there is bad fruit from this person's work ethic. On the other hand, when a person habitually uses personal freedom to add quality and value to a situation, one can observe good fruit from their work ethic.

In a highly controlled environment the leader never has the opportunity to observe how a person is internally guided. Too often, we discover how a person is internally motivated after we have promoted them to a place of more freedom and less supervision.

Day 9

"A wrathful man stirreth up strife: but he that is slow to anger appeaseth strife." Proverbs 15:18

Angry people promote anger. They force otherwise calm and peaceful people to wrath. A part of leadership development is helping the potential leader work through their unresolved issues. A person with power and unresolved issues is a dangerous person. His environment becomes the place where he expresses the emotions related to those issues. There are many unresolved issues that drive people to pursue positions of power and prestige. Ego, low self-worth, money and control are just a few. It is those very issues, however, that bring about their destruction once they have reached their position of power.

A common negative emotion in ministers is anger. The anger can be a result of personal issues or negative experiences in the ministry. Anger, however, becomes a blinding, destructive force that creates the very situations we fear. Proverbs has a lot to say about the fruit of an angry person. Proverbs 25:23 says, *"The north wind driveth away rain: so doth an angry countenance a backbiting tongue."* Just as surely as the wind drives rain, anger will drive backbiting.

In Proverbs 14:7 it says, *"He that is soon angry dealeth foolishly."* Anger drives a man to impulsive, irrational behavior. Anger turns small situations into big ones. When we find ourselves angry we should ask, "Why am I angry? Am I angry because someone really did me wrong or because they didn't live up to my expectations?" Very often we find ourselves upset over things that have nothing to do with us. Yet, anger, when unchecked, drives

149

us to foolish perceptions and actions.

Anger is such a negative, destructive emotion that we are warned to have nothing to do with an angry person. *"Make no friendship with an angry man; and with a furious man thou shalt not go: Lest thou learn his ways, and get a snare to thy soul."* Proverbs 22:24-25. The angry person will soon make us angry.

At one time I realized that I was becoming negative and sarcastic. I began to have and "edge" to my preaching. I felt agitated in my own soul. I could not understand what had happened to me. In time, I realized that I had taken the offense of a close friend. His unresolved anger toward the church subtly, but powerfully, affected my emotions. After all attempts to minister to this person failed, I ultimately had to follow the wisdom of this scripture. I departed from the angry person and my anger departed.

Day 10

"An inheritance may be gotten hastily at the beginning; but the end thereof shall not be blessed." Proverbs 10:21

The fulfillment of our call is the inheritance every leader longs for. We all want success today. It is healthy and natural to want to do it all now, yet, maturity tempers and wisdom guides us to a place where those emotions that drive us to succeed today are focused in a healthy, productive way. Personal development helps us to see time as an ally instead of an enemy.

The person that has to have it all today is driven by something unhealthy. Proverbs says he has an *"evil eye."* That need for success **NOW** can cause us to take short cuts that will rob us of true success. We can find ourselves in the sin we hoped to help others overcome. *"Also, that the soul be without knowledge, it is not good; and he that hasteth with his feet sinneth."* Proverbs 19:2. Just as surely as prosperity destroys, foolish impatience will lead us down a path we do not want to walk. *"The thoughts of the diligent tend only to plenteousness; but of every one that is hasty only to want."* Proverbs 21:5.

The hasty person creates havoc and loses the ability to see what is obvious to all. *"He that is hasty of spirit exalteth folly."* Proverbs 14:29. *"A faithful man shall abound with blessings: but he that maketh haste to be rich shall not be innocent."* Proverbs 28:20.

Over the years I have observed that many of those

who got the fastest start faced the most pain. They did not allow themselves time to grow with the process. They were forced to make decisions that were beyond their experience. The very goal that they thought would bring them joy only brought pain. Yet, I have seen those who with patience and persistence followed the call of God, grow and prosper year by year like an oak tree.

Day 11

"A good name is rather to be chosen than great riches, and loving favour rather than silver and gold." Proverbs 22:1

When I was young I saw little value in having a good name. Because of that lack of wisdom I live with accusations to this very day. I have to accept my part in making those accusations believable, whether they are true or not. Too often, we think it is enough to prove an accusation to be true or false. The real challenge is living a life that makes an accusation unbelievable. There will always be accusers. We can never stop them. Our responsibility is to live above reproach.

There is another aspect of maintaining a good name. Sometimes we must choose whether we will strive for the favor of the religious community or to those we seek to reach and serve. As a wider gap grows between the church and the world it becomes increasingly difficult to keep both groups happy. History reveals that very few people have been able to develop relevant ministry to their generation and maintain the approval of the religious community. Sadly, the church is often more concerned about maintaining religious tradition than reaching our society.

In such a situation, one must live above reproach while suffering reproach. We must conduct ourselves in a way to maintain effectiveness with those who need God. Waymon Rodgers, built a very large church in Louisville, Kentucky. I had the privilege of meeting and ministering with him shortly before his death. I found this to be an interesting comment made by one of his church members, "In all of the church's growth and expansion, Brother Rodgers never pushed ahead at the destruction of others. He kept a good name in the community."

Not one sinner showed up at Jesus' trial to bring accusation against Him. It was only those who had their religious views challenged. In all things, seek not to offend. But if offense must come, let it come from those

151

who know God. They have the resources to work it out if they choose. Never offend those who do not know God. We may be their last stop before eternity.

John Maxwell says, "Image is what people think we are, Integrity is what we really are." Those who are overly concerned with image are more concerned with how it looks than how it is. Those who are concerned with integrity seek to preserve a good name, yet are more satisfied with a good conscience.

Day 12

"A prudent man foreseeth the evil, and hideth himself: but the simple pass on, and are punished." Proverbs 23:3

As a reactionary society we tend to act too late on the wrong information, failing to accomplish the desired results. Leaders cannot be reactive; they must be proactive. How they respond to situations must be the product of "who they are in Christ." Every leader must have an emotional anchor that keeps them stable in the most troubled waters.

The unstable leader judges events in a subjective manner. He assumes that everything is a reflection on his personal identity. Therefore, he fails to see the larger picture. He creates chaos when there is none. Proverbs says that the wicked flees when no one pursues. The righteous, on the other hand, are as bold as a lion.[3] The bold leader does not need to prove his position. He observes life with a clear mind.

Because he views life in an objective manner he is able to foresee the unfolding of events, interpret them properly and act accordingly. He knows when to "run" and he knows when to stand. He knows how to seek the proper protection (action). The simple leader is always in chaos. He fails to foresee and plan his strategies. He is like a man who waits until he is thirsty to dig the well.

Likewise, the prudent leader foresees opportunities. He foresees the trends of his community and seizes the opportunity to minister effectively. He is not bound by religious tradition. His need for approval does not dictate his actions.

The ability to foresee is found in a peaceful nature. The proactive leader develops the ability to respond calmly

---

[3] Proverbs 28:1.

152

NOTES

to every situation. He is not driven to extremes by uncontrollable emotions and impulses. He foresees and prepares!

Day 13

"He that oppresseth the poor to increase his riches, and he that giveth to the rich, shall surely come to want." Proverbs 22:16

The leader always has the wealth of knowledge, experience and opportunity. The poor in spirit come to find help and encouragement. The leader who takes advantage of those who look to him for help is like one who oppresses the poor for his personal gain. In the end, he will never see what he truly desires.

The compassionate leader has an empathetic heart. He has compassion for the pain and oppression of the people. He understands, and handles with the greatest of priority, his position of influence with the people. He is always aware of his influence and never uses that power for financial or emotional gain. The Word of God gives the strongest rebuke for the shepherd who grows fat at the expense of the flock.

For too many years the church has bred contempt for people. We only have value for the lost if they get saved. Then we only value the saved if they do all that we expect of them. When one has no value for any group or individual, he is unfit to minister to them. The quality of ministry offered is closely linked to the value we hold for the people. Moreover, one will always abuse those for whom they have low esteem.

The compassionate leader surrounds himself with those who hold all people in high esteem. Every human being, saved or lost, is equal to the value of the life of Christ. He recognizes that a part of his influence should be used to convey that value to all.

Day 14

"These things also belong to the wise. It is not good to have respect of persons in judgment. He that saith unto the wicked, Thou art righteous; him shall the people curse, nations shall abhor him: But to them that rebuke him shall be delight, and a good blessing shall come upon them. Every man shall kiss his lips that giveth a right answer." Proverbs 24:23-26

The effective leader never assumes the role of a judge. He recognizes that judgement belongs only to the Lord. Only a corrupt leader would honor the wicked and oppress the righteous. Yet, when one assumes judgement, this often occurs unknowingly.

The Bible never gives us the right to judge. It gives us the directive to observe fruit. We never know why people do what they do, we only know what they do. All I really know about you are your actions. The moment I add anything to that, whether good or bad, I have entered into judgement.

Judgement looks for who is guilty and who should be punished. In our works mentality we feel the need to justify all of our actions. Therefore, if I love you and desire to show that love, I feel the need to justify my actions by judging you worthy.

The person who needs justifications for their actions does not grasp the love of God. We need not declare someone righteous to justify our kindness. We need not declare someone unrighteous to justify our unwillingness to do what they desire of us.

Our actions should be governed by our freedom of choice and observance of the facts. If I do not want to help you do something, I need not condemn you to justify my choice. Too often, we see the fruit and begin to judge. Even when we see the fruit, we really do not know the motive of the heart, nor do we need to know.

The correct answer for the benevolent leader is, "I will give you the love of God whether you do or do not deserve it."

Day 15

"Prepare thy work without, and make it fit for thyself in the field; and afterwards build thine house." Proverbs 24:27

The law of reinvestment is essential for the one who desires true success. In the beginning of any great venture it is essential to invest and reinvest. The farmer knows that if he eats his seed he will live for one more season. If he plants his seed, however, he will live for years.

A leader must be willing to invest in that which creates perpetuation. In this day of "instant gratification" few people have the heart to pioneer and develop a ministry or a department within a ministry. There is the tendency to eat the seed, build the house and neglect the field. It is a basic self-centered attitude, driven by the need for instant gratification.

While the laborer is certainly worthy of his hire, be careful not to take so much today that you destroy the success of tomorrow. Be cautious with those who are not willing to first do that which perpetuates the opportunity.

There is much pressure to prove your faith by living the highlife. As the glamour mentality has overtaken the church, many ministers have sacrificed the work of their hands in a vain attempt to gain the illusion of success. The truly visionary leader recognizes that the sacrifices made today will pay dividends for a lifetime.

Day 16

"As an earring of gold, and an ornament of fine gold, so is a wise reprover upon an obedient ear." Proverbs 25:12

The wise leader uses great discretion in reproof. He recognizes the vanity in attempting to teach or correct the foolish. He knows that a foolish person will not learn by instruction or correction. The unteachable will occasionally learn by suffering the consequences of their actions. *"Judgments are prepared for scorners, and stripes for the back of fools."* Proverbs 19:29.

In the parable of the prodigal son, the loving father allowed his son to experience the fruit of his actions. I am sure he felt great pain watching his son live in complete foolishness, yet, he was wise enough not to interrupt the process. Only when his son reached the place of living in the undeniable consequences of his actions did he "come to himself." Like the loving father in this parable, the wise leader knows that he should save his reproof for the hearing ear and must allow the unteachable to learn from the consequences.

The contentious and foolish leader contends with those who take no delight in learning. Their delight is in being right. Thus, he is consumed with contention and strife. In the end, he feels the Gospel does not work. He becomes bitter toward all people.

The wise leader gives himself to those who have demonstrated a desire and willingness to learn. Therefore, his effort is not in vain. They sow their seeds in good ground that bring forth a bountiful harvest.

Day 17

"By long forbearing is a prince persuaded, and a soft tongue breaketh the bone." Proverbs 25:15

Only a brute attempts to move another individual or a group of people by force. Just like the law of physics that states, force creates an opposing power equal to or greater than itself.[4] It is the beginning of conflict. A skillful communicator is patient and forbearing. The loving leader has the other person's good as a priority equal to their own.

Most people will do almost anything, within reason, if they can find a way to do it and feel comfortable. Therefore, a skilled negotiator always approaches a person in a way that makes them feel comfortable. He is very careful to never violate the person's sense of self-worth.

It is only a good deal when everyone wins. This happens only when everyone involved walks away from a decision with peace and a sense of gain. Therefore, the wise communicator relies on gentle persuasion instead of force.

Day 18

"Iron sharpeneth iron; so a man sharpeneth the countenance of his friend." Proverbs 27:17

Secure leaders surround themselves with those who can challenge and instruct. He recognizes and welcomes the opportunity to be taught by his team members. Personal growth and effective leadership are more important than maintaining the appearance of supremacy. A secure leader recognizes that personal growth becomes stagnant when surrounded by those who are of equal or inferior abilities.

It takes a wide variety of strengths to form an effective team. If all team members are alike it is doubtful that there is enough variety. If everyone sees everything the same way, then you do not have a team; you have clones.

The confident person is surrounded, when possible, with those who have superior skills. He trusts the Word of God that says, *"He that walketh with wise men shall be wise: but a companion of fools shall be destroyed."* Proverbs 13:20. He is hungry for the input and wisdom of

---

[4] Emotional force becomes multiplied through the people it effects. As Jesus said, it comes back pressed down, shaken together and running over. It never comes back in the same amount.

those who have greater knowledge and experience.

Every inferior team member becomes a weight around the neck of the leader. Rather than leading a team of people who have the skills needed to do the job. The insecure leader has to carry all the weight. Every decision falls to his desk. He soon wearies from the load.

An effective team should not depend on the leader for the answers; they should depend on him for leadership and facilitation of the goals. The head of every department should know more about that department than the senior leader. Leadership, after all, is not superiority. It does not come from power, but humility.

Leaders lead people, not tasks. The superior leader is superior in people skills. His strength is in leading those who are superior at the task. He takes all of the individual strengths and skills and brings them together into one congruent effort of synergy whereby all become greater than they could be on their own. He leads the people. The people accomplish the tasks.

Day 19

"If a wise man contendeth with a foolish man, whether he rage or laugh, there is no rest." Proverbs 29:9

This word "contend" strongly indicates an attempt to "set right." The immature and self-righteous see it as their responsibility to set people right. The word "contends," presupposes the passing of judgement. Before setting someone right we must judge them to be wrong. Then we must assume that we are right. Then we must violate every sane law of communication.

Proverbs 20:3 says, *"It is an honour for a man to cease from strife: but every fool will be meddling."* It is foolish to meddle. One who desires to set others right is a meddler. He creates strife and conflict. He brings a reproach to himself and the organization. As I teach my staff, "The one who contends with a fool is the greater fool."

It may be good to develop a personal checklist before confronting. Ask yourself the following questions and you may achieve much greater results with much more peace:

1. Am I confronting for my benefit or the benefit of another?

2. Am I in a positive, peaceful frame of mind, or am I acting from anger or impatience?
3. Will the way I am planning to handle this promote peace or strife?
4. Am I doing this just to prove that I am right?
5. Am I trying to get in the last word?
6. Does this person have a history of being approachable, teachable and reasonable?

2 Timothy 2:23 says, "*Don't have anything to do with foolish and stupid arguments, because you know they produce quarrels.*" NIV. Most arguments are stupid. They are especially stupid when we know they will produce more strife.

Day 20

"*A fool uttereth all his mind: but a wise man keepeth it in till afterwards.*" Proverbs 29:11

The idealistic, immature leader feels that he should "lay all the cards on the table" up front. He assumes that everyone thinks the way he thinks. He has little awareness or respect for how the other person processes information. Additionally, when all the information he has laid out is used against him, he feels victimized.

When we give out too much information too fast we run the risk of overwhelming the other person. We have had time to think through our position. We have considered all the options and possibilities. Too often we expect others to "take our word for it." We fail to allow them the same opportunity we had to process the situation.

A wise communicator seeks to understand how the other person desires to receive communication. That person is then approached in the manner most effective with them. They are given small amounts of information and allowed time to process and evaluate what they have heard. As we receive feedback and questions we perceive the appropriate time to move forward with more information.

The need to speak our entire mind can spring from several negative sources. It can spring from the need to prove ourselves right in the beginning, which reflects a state of inflexibility. It can reflect an egotistic attitude that delights in airing its own opinions. It is an indication for a lack of concern for another's point of view, but it is clearly a lack of trust in one of God's directives for effective

158

communication.

Day 21

"If a ruler hearken to lies, all his servants are wicked."
Proverbs 29:12

I like the way this reads in *The Amplified Bible* *"If a ruler listens to falsehood, all his officials will be wicked."*[5] The leader who does not have a system for developing and observing his staff never knows if the information he receives is truth or error. He has no system of checks and balances.

People around a leader adapt to his system. The Romans say, "Like the king, like the people." People soon learn how the game is played and follow suit.[6] In the absence of an effective leadership program, the naïve leader usually begins listening to lies unintentionally. Over time, the people around him lose confidence in the leader and either leave or become corrupt.

Too often, we listen to lies because they are what we want to believe. I had a conversation with a staff member of a very large church. At the height of success, they began a building program that ultimately became the downfall of the church. Because of what seemed to be a need to impress his peers, the pastor wanted to build a very large building. His staff advised him against such a large building.

Since they were not saying what he wanted to hear he began to surround himself with "yes men," those that were quick to agree with the leader. They said what he wanted to hear. They did not aggressively lie; they simply agreed with a leader who had the wrong facts. In time, the new building was built, they never filled it, the church fell into financial disarray and lost all of its effectiveness. The lies to which we fall prey may be the ones we tell!

Day 22

"Where there is no vision, the people perish: but he that keepeth the law, happy is he." Proverbs 29:18

A true leader always has a clear objective in mind.

---

[5] *The Amplified Bible*, Zondervan Bible Publishers, Grand Rapids
[6] *The Expositor's Bible Commentary*, Volume 5, Zondervan Publishing House, Grand Rapids

He is able to link every action, every program and every decision to the accomplishment of the goal. He is not satisfied by the mere flurry of pointless activities.

Equally important, an effective leader is able to communicate the vision in a way that stirs the passions of others. The ability to communicate the vision, stir others to passion, yet never make people feel pressured, is the mark of a great leader.

Motivation is when I stir you to do what you want to do. Manipulation is when I stir you to do what I want you to do. It is essential that every person be stirred to fulfill the vision while maintaining his or her personal goals and dreams. People do not perish because they lose the vision I attempt to give them. They perish when they lose their personal vision.

Day 23

"He that delicately bringeth up his servant from a child shall have him become his son at the length." Proverbs 29:21

Because we are people of extremes we tend to either give too much mercy or demand too much. The result of sowing extremes is reaping extremes. We want a relationship with those around us that have the warmth of family and the professionalism needed for the situation. It is seldom we find this blend in our own children, much less those with whom we labor.

If we raise a person up in delicacy, they not only become a son; they become a spoiled son. Strong's indicates that the word "son" refers to a thankless son. People who are always allowed to live in the exception are always thankless. Whether we realize it or not, they are usually manipulating our emotions.

Every organization must have standards. When people do not uphold those standards they should never lose our love, friendship and acceptance; but they should lose their position. We do not want a staff of legalists. We do, however, want a staff that has a high sense of integrity and personal commitment.

Too often, we fail to walk circumspectly in the place of friend and leader. When my friendship prevents me from leading you I can no longer be your leader. When I can no longer correct you for fear of the loss of friendship, the situation is out of control. People of character can be friends and maintain a professional relationship.

We do not need thankless sons as staff members. Remember, the spoiled child was spoiled by his parents. Likewise, the spoiled staff member is a product of leadership. Love as a father; lead as a king.

Day 24

"For three things the earth is disquieted, and for four which it cannot bear: For a servant when he reigneth; and a fool when he is filled with meat." Proverbs 30:21-22

There is a difference between a servant and a slave. We are set free from slavery in Christ. We do not serve God to earn righteousness or acceptance. The legalist serves for a price. He has an expectation from God for his service and he has an expectation from his leader.

Hebrews 12:15 teaches that the root of bitterness is the result of "falling from grace." Falling from grace occurs when we enter the realm of works. The performance-oriented person becomes bitter when their works do not bring them what they feel they deserve. Their bitterness becomes a divisive poison whereby many are defiled.

Paul taught the principle of a "love servant." A love servant is someone who recognizes they have freedom, yet, their love compels them to serve. This should be the mentality of the servant of God. He should have a revelation of their freedom from works for righteousness. That revelation should produce such an overwhelming sense of appreciation that they desire to serve.

One of the keys to avoiding division is to never allow a person with a works mentality (a slave) to rule. When the codependent lays down his life for the leader, there will always be a payment due. When you fail to make that unexpected payment in the form of a promotion, a staff position, public recognition or personal loyalty, you will pay a tremendous price.

Day 25

"There be three things which go well, yea, four are comely in going: A lion which is strongest among beasts, and turneth not away for any; A greyhound; an he goat also; and a king, against whom there is no rising up." Proverbs 30:29-31

161

Every leader desires freedom from an uprising. Too often, we think we secure our position by power. As I have observed many ministries over the last 25 years, I have seen that it is not those who are strong in power that remain free from the threat of uprising. Instead, it is those leaders who are strong in love and mercy. Being strong in the Lord is for the purpose of victory not control.

If I depend on power, intelligence, wit or any other factor for my security I will never be secure. There will always be someone stronger, smarter and wittier than I. Even when those traits cause one to prevail, they seldom deter an uprising.

Walk in integrity. Let your life be motivated by love. Preach the truth; yet, temper all that you do with mercy. You will reap what you sow. The man of power can stop an uprising. The man of love and mercy does not have an uprising.

Day 26

"He who guards his lips guards his life, but he who speaks rashly will come to ruin." Proverbs 13:3, NIV.

The words of a leader carry weight. Unlike the words of others, they can crush the heart or create expectation with no intention to do either. The leader who thinks aloud will cry aloud. It is essential that a leader have control over his mouth.

Proverbs 21:23 says, *"Whoso keepeth his mouth and his tongue keepeth his soul from troubles."* Careless words have caused unbelievable amounts of strife and pain. The discerning leader is always aware of his company. He never loses sight of what is appropriate in the setting.

The foolish leader places the burden of responsibility on the hearer. "They should not interpret it that way. That is not what I meant." is the cry of those who are hasty with their words. Words are not on loan, they are given. Once dished out they cannot be taken back.

Day 27

"The wise in heart shall be called prudent: and the sweetness of the lips increaseth learning." Proverbs 16:21

The Bible says to "speak the truth in love." God, in His wisdom, wanted us to understand that it is not just the

NOTES

truth that affects others, but the way that truth is presented. Too often, the desired affect of our sermons, corrections and encouragement is lost to the way we serve it.

Proverbs 16:23-24 continues, *"The heart of the wise teacheth his mouth, and addeth learning to his lips. Pleasant words are as an honeycomb, sweet to the soul, and health to the bones."* The wise leader makes learning a joy. The words are made sweet. His desire to heal tempers his words. The intention of his heart directs his mouth.

Angry words stir up strife. Words spoken from superiority create debate. Words of obligation engender resistance. Legalism breeds criticism. Pleasant words make learning a joy. People will receive nearly anything we say - if we can make it pleasant.

Day 28

"The heart of the righteous studieth to answer: but the mouth of the wicked poureth out evil things." Proverbs 15:28

A hasty answer promotes sin. Too often, our need to answer leads us to lie. Usually, when a leader lies, it is not a blatant desire to deceive. It comes from the inability to answer the question appropriately. The wise leader studies his answer.

We are not obligated to answer every question. So often, when Jesus was asked a question, He never answered. In many cases, His answer would have brought about His arrest or immediate death at the hands of the people. Yet, He did not feel obligated to answer every question. Jesus often answered a question with a question.

Proverbs says, *"the multitude of words lacks not for sin."* The person who cannot answer honestly, without incriminating himself, will talk around the issue until he lies. People will bear no answer, but they will not tolerate lies.

Learn to answer wisely. Learn when to answer and when not to answer. Always give an appropriate answer or refuse to answer, but do it tactfully. It is better to be seen as a man who will not answer than a man who lies. *"Excellent speech becometh not a fool: much less do lying lips a prince."* Proverbs 17:7.

One of the greatest motivators for lying is the loss of approval. *"The fear of man bringeth a snare: but whoso putteth his trust in the LORD shall be safe."* Proverbs 29:25. The fear of man usually manifests as the fear of rejection. Too often, our lies are not outright, they are just a "mild slant on the truth." The person who slants the truth for acceptance has a self-worth problem that has grown into a lying problem.

Confident leaders recognize the impossibility of pleasing everyone or being liked by everyone. Some will approve and some will always disapprove. However, exaggeration is never a suitable option for improving our image.

Day 29

"In the multitude of words there wanteth not sin: but he that refraineth his lips is wise." Proverbs 10:19

We do not know all the answers. We are not always right. Even if we were it would still be better to speak less and listen more. As someone has said, "I already know everything I know. If I listen I can learn what you know."

The Amplified Bible talks about the fool who delights in airing his opinions and delights in revealing himself. The leader that will be respected is the one who listens as much as he talks. The man who listens is considered wise. Moreover, he is wise. He is wise enough to honor others by valuing their opinions. He gains insight from the life experience of others.

Much time is wasted in ministry shooting at the wrong target. One does not actually know how to minister until he has listened. Until we have listened we are operating from assumption and judgement. A minister who does not listen is like a doctor who does not diagnose. He simply cuts you open and looks for the problem.

A failure to listen makes many negative statements. It says, "I don't care about you." It says, "Your view is not important." It says, "I am going to proceed with my plan regardless of your desires." It says, "I am going to do all the talking." According to the Word of God that will always lead us into sin.

Relationships are difficult at best. Leaders are in the most difficult kind of relationship. We have the task of leading others where they are usually afraid to go. We must maintain their trust. We must help them fulfill their dreams. There is much room for misunderstanding. Misunderstandings are more often the result of not listening than not being able to comprehend.

The more I listen, the less likely I will wander into sin. The more I listen, the more I convey my concern and interest for you. The listener grows wiser and wiser. Even if he does not grow wiser, he is viewed as wiser. *"Even a fool, when he holdeth his peace, is counted wise: and he that shutteth his lips is esteemed a man of understanding."* Proverbs 17:28.

Day 30

"The mouth of a righteous man is a well of life." Proverbs 10:11. "In the lips of him that hath understanding wisdom is found." Proverbs 10:13. "The tongue of the just is as choice silver: the heart of the wicked is little worth. The lips of the righteous feed many." Proverbs 10:20-21.

The Book of James tells us that teachers will be judged more harshly. I do not feel it is speaking of judgement from God, but judgement from people. It goes on to say that the person who can control his words is perfect.

Controlling our words is not the painful result of personal scrutiny and introspection. Controlling our words is the result of our clearly established intentions. What is our intention? Do we want our words to feed, bless, heal and encourage, or do we want our words to glorify us?

When the captain of a ship makes a commitment to a destination, he then takes the wheel and guides the ship from that intention. When we make the intention to give life, our communication style is set on course. All of our actions are a reflection, to a great degree, of our intentions.

The person who intends to be a life giver is empowered by the grace of God. His words and actions flow from a heart that is set on a course. The person who always struggles with their words is being guided by the destination they have chosen. Failure to choose one is a choice for the other. Life is easy when we have chosen our destination and committed our way to the Lord.